STUDENT COOKBOOK 2025

Easy, Quick, Budget-Friendly Hungry Student Recipes to Prepare for All with Photos

EILEEN BOND

TABLE OF CONTENTS

Hey there, future kitchen champion! First things first – take a deep breath. If you're holding this cookbook, you're probably experiencing one of two emotions: excitement about your newfound kitchen freedom, or mild panic about having to cook for yourself. Maybe both? Well, you're in the right place either way.

I remember my first week at university like it was yesterday. There I was, standing in my tiny student kitchen, staring at a pot of what was supposed to be pasta but somehow turned into a sticky, gluey mess. My flat mates still joke about the fire alarm incident with the toast (pro tip: that smoke sensitivity setting is there for a reason). But you know what? Every kitchen disaster taught me something, and now I'm here to help you skip the trial-and-error phase and jump straight to making meals you'll actually want to eat.

This cookbook is different from those glossy, Instagram-perfect recipe books you might have flipped through. You won't find any calls for truffle oil or fancy kitchen gadgets here. What you will find is real food that fits into real student life – meals you can cook when you're running late for a lecture, recipes that won't blow your entire week's budget, and dishes that will impress your flat mates (and maybe that special someone) without requiring a master's degree in culinary arts.

We've organized everything with your lifestyle in mind. Need a quick breakfast before that 9 AM lecture? Got it. Looking for meals you can prep on Sunday and eat all week? Check. Want to host a dinner party without having a nervous breakdown? We've got your back. There's even a special chapter dedicated to "hangover helpers" (not that we're encouraging anything, but let's be realistic here).

The best part? Every recipe has been tested in actual student kitchens, with their temperamental ovens, shared fridges, and that one stovetop burner that never quite works right. We've included substitutions for when the shops are closed, shortcuts for when you're running late, and tips for making the most of your limited kitchen space and equipment.

Whether you're a complete kitchen newbie who thinks boiling water is advanced cooking, or someone who's ready to level up their culinary game, this book will meet you where you are. Remember, everyone starts somewhere, and by the end of your first term, you'll be amazed at how far you've come from those instant noodle days.

So grab your apron (or let's be honest, your cleanest t-shirt), and let's get cooking. Your journey to becoming a confident cook starts here, and trust me – if I could learn to make more than just toast, anyone can.

Alright, future food wizard, let's get you set up! I know what you're thinking – "Do I really need all this stuff?" After spending three years in student accommodation (and making every equipment mistake possible), I can tell you exactly what's worth your precious budget and what's just going to collect dust in your cupboard.

Here's the thing about student cooking: it's like building a character in a video game. You start with the basic equipment (your starter pack), and as you level up, you add more tools to your arsenal. No need to raid the kitchen department all at once – let's break it down into what you actually need.

The Student Kitchen Starter Pack

Think of this as your essential survival kit. These are the items that will transform you from a pot noodle novice to a capable cook:

The Core Five (Start Here!)

1. A Quality Chef's Knife (£20-30)
-This is your kitchen MVP
-Look for a 8-inch/20cm blade
-Brands like Victorinox offer great student-budget options
-Trust me, those £5 knife sets are a false economy
2. Two Chopping Boards (£10-15)
-One for raw meat (plastic, dishwasher safe)
-One for everything else (wood or plastic)
-Pro tip: get different colors to avoid mix-ups
3. Large Non-stick Frying Pan (£15-25)
-28cm is the sweet spot for size
- Skip the super cheap ones – they'll lose their non-stick faster than your student loan disappears
- Look for oven-safe handles if possible
4. Medium Saucepan with Lid (£12-20)
- Around 3-liter capacity is perfect
- Must have a lid (trust me, your pasta water will boil faster)
- Great for soups, pasta, rice, and late-night pot noodles
5. Measuring Implements (£5-10)
- At least one measuring jug
- A set of spoons (trust me, "a spoonful" is not a universal measurement)
- Top tip: your phone can double as a kitchen scale with the right app

The Why-These-Five?

I picked these specific items because they'll handle about 80% of everything you'll cook as a student. You can make a proper meal with just these tools – from a basic stir-fry to a decent pasta dish. Plus, they're all items that will last beyond your student years if you treat them right. Think of this list as your kitchen foundation. Just like you wouldn't start a degree without a laptop and notebooks, you shouldn't start cooking without these basics. And hey, they make great items to add to your birthday wishlist if the budget is tight!

ESSENTIAL EQUIPMENT LIST

The Absolute Basics (Start Here)
- A Good Sharp Knife: Your most important tool. One quality chef's knife is better than a set of cheap ones. Budget around £20-30 for this - it's worth it.
- Chopping Board: Get two if possible - one for raw meat and one for everything else.
- Large Non-stick Frying Pan: For everything from stir-fries to pancakes.
- Medium Saucepan with Lid: Perfect for pasta, rice, and soups.
- Measuring Cups/Spoons: Because "a handful" isn't always the right amount.
- Can Opener: Trust me, you don't want to be without this.
- Colander: For draining pasta and washing vegetables.
- Level Up Items (Get These When You Can)
- Microwave-Safe Container Set: Essential for leftovers and meal prep.
- Baking Sheet: For roasting vegetables, making cookies, and sheet pan dinners.
- Wooden Spoons: At least two - they're gentle on non-stick surfaces.
- Grater: For cheese, vegetables, and more.
- Kitchen Scissors: Surprisingly useful for everything from cutting herbs to opening packages.

Nice to Have (But Not Essential)
- Blender: Great for smoothies and soups, but wait for sales.
- Rice Cooker: A lifesaver if you eat lots of rice.
- Food Scale: Helpful for baking and portion control.
- Hand Mixer: For baking enthusiasts.

UNDERSTANDING YOUR COOKING SPACE

Making the Most of a Small Kitchen

Student kitchens are notorious for being, well, compact. Here's how to make it work:

Vertical Storage Solutions
- Use command hooks on walls for utensils
- Install over-the-door organizers
- Stack containers efficiently in cupboards
- Use magnetic strips for knife storage

Counter Space Management
- Create a fold-down workspace with a wall-mounted table
- Use a cutting board over the sink for extra prep space
- Keep frequently used items in a caddy that can be moved easily
- Clean as you go - it's essential in small spaces

Shared Kitchen Survival Guide

Living with others? Here's how to make it work:

Storage Strategies
- Label everything with your name and date
- Use different colored containers for each person
- Keep valuable items in your room if necessary
- Consider a mini-fridge if sharing is problematic

Communal Kitchen Etiquette
- Create a cleaning rota and stick to it
- Agree on shared basics (washing up liquid, paper towels)

- Set guidelines for borrowing items/ingredients
- Establish quiet hours for late-night cooking

KITCHEN BASICS

Listen up, kitchen rookies! Before we dive into fancy recipes and culinary adventures, let's talk about the basics that will keep you from setting off the fire alarm (speaking from experience here). Think of this as your 'Kitchen 101' crash course – the stuff that seems obvious to seasoned cooks but nobody actually tells you when you're starting out.

The Holy Trinity of Cooking Safety

1. Temperature Control

Look, I learned this the hard way – not everything needs to be cooked on maximum heat! Here's your cheat sheet:

- High Heat (7-9 on electric hobs): For bringing water to boil and quick stir-fries
- Medium Heat (4-6): Your go-to for most cooking
- Low Heat (1-3): For simmering sauces and keeping things warm
- Smoking pan = danger zone! If you see smoke, turn it down before your dinner becomes charcoal

2. Cross-Contamination Prevention

This isn't just chef talk – it's about not getting food poisoning during exam week:

- Raw meat gets its own chopping board (the red one, traditionally)
- Wash hands after touching raw meat (yes, every single time)
- Don't use the same tongs for raw and cooked food
- When in doubt, wash it out!

3. Sharp Knife Safety

A sharp knife is actually safer than a dull one (counterintuitive, I know!):

- Keep fingers tucked while chopping (think cat paw position)
- Let falling knives fall (never try to catch them!)
- Keep your knife clean and sharp
- No knife fights in the kitchen (yes, this needs to be said)

Essential Cooking Methods Every Student Should Know

The Big Four:

1. Boiling
- Water should be bubbling like a jacuzzi
- Salt your pasta water (it should taste like the sea)
- Don't overcrowd the pot (your pasta needs space to dance)

2. Frying
- Heat the pan BEFORE adding oil
- Listen for the sizzle
- Resist the urge to constantly stir (let those veggies get some color!)

3. Roasting
- Preheat your oven (seriously, don't skip this)
- Line your baking tray (foil is your friend)
- Space your items out (crowded trays = steamed not roasted)

4. Microwaving
- Yes, it's a legitimate cooking method!
- Use microwave-safe containers (metal = fireworks show)
- Cover your food (unless you enjoy cleaning exploded beans off the ceiling)

FOOD SAFETY AND HYGIENE

Let's talk about keeping your kitchen from becoming a science experiment (unless that's what you're studying!). After witnessing one too many fuzzy discoveries in shared fridges and surviving a legendary case of questionable curry, I'm here to share the non-negotiable rules of kitchen cleanliness.

The Golden Rules of Kitchen Hygiene

Hands Are Everything
- Wash them for 20 seconds (sing 'Happy Birthday' twice)
- Always wash after:
  - Touching raw meat/fish
  - Using the bathroom (obviously!)
  - Handling garbage
  - Touching your phone (yes, that thing is dirty)
- Keep hand soap by the kitchen sink (that body wash from your shower doesn't count)

Cross-Contamination: The Silent Kitchen Villain

Think of your kitchen like a crime scene – you don't want evidence spreading around!
- Color-coding is your friend:
  - Red boards = raw meat
  - Green = veggies
  - Blue = cooked food
  - White = ready-to-eat
- Use separate tea towels for:
  - Hand drying
  - Dish drying
  - Surface wiping
- Change them weekly (or immediately if they get that funky smell)

Fridge Management 101

Remember that milk that turned into cheese (and not in a good way)? Let's prevent that:
- Top shelf: Ready-to-eat foods
- Middle: Dairy products
- Bottom: Raw meat (to prevent drips)
- Drawers: Fruits and veggies
- Ideal temperature: 5°C or below (get a cheap fridge thermometer)

The "When In Doubt" Rules
- If it's furry and it's not blue cheese, bin it
- Smell test isn't foolproof (some nasties are odorless)
- "Best before" ≠ "poison after" (use common sense)
- "Use by" = actually follow this one
- If your flatmate says "it's probably fine," it probably isn't

Quick Clean Routine (5 Minutes, No Excuses)

1. Wipe surfaces (actual cleaner, not just water!)
2. Clean spills immediately (dried pasta sauce = archaeological dig)
3. Do dishes after every meal (morning-you will thank evening-you)
4. Empty bin when full (or when mysterious smells appear)
5. Sweep floor quickly (those pasta pieces will attract unwanted roommates)

BUDGETING AND SHOPPING

Let's talk money, honey! After blowing half my first term's budget on takeaways (and living on beans for the remaining weeks), I learned a thing or two about smart food shopping. Consider this your ultimate guide to eating well without breaking the bank.

The Smart Shopping Strategy

Timing Is Everything
- Evening Bargains: Hit shops an hour before closing for reduced items
  - Yellow sticker items = your new best friends
  - Most reductions happen between 7-8 PM
  - Freeze what you won't eat immediately
- Mid-week Shopping: Less crowded, better deals
- Avoid Shopping When Hungry: Trust me, you don't need three types of cookies

Supermarket Hierarchy

Not all shops are created equal! Here's your cost-saving route:
1. Budget Supermarkets (Aldi, Lidl)
- Basics and staples
- Fresh produce
- Generic brands
2. Regular Supermarkets (Tesco, Asda)
- Special offers
- Student discount days
- Specific brands you can't live without
3. Express/Local Stores
- Emergency items only
- Usually 20-30% more expensive
- Late-night desperate purchases

The Student Stockpile

Essential items that won't blow your budget:
- Carbs: Rice, pasta, noodles (buy in bulk)
- Proteins: Tinned beans, chickpeas, tuna
- Freezer Friends: Mixed veg, frozen chicken, berries
- Long-life Heroes: Tinned tomatoes, stock cubes, spices

Money-Saving Masterclass

The Golden Rules
1. Never Shop Without a List
- Plan meals in advance
- Check what you already have
- Stick to the list (those chocolate offers are traps!)
2. Buy in Bulk Wisely
- Split bulk buys with flatmates
- Calculate price per unit
- Only bulk buy what you'll actually use
3. Generic Brands Are Your Friends
- Basic range pasta tastes the same

- Save fancy brands for ingredients where it matters
- Do blind taste tests – you'll be surprised!

Student Discount Hacks
- Get an NUS/Student Beans card
- Download supermarket apps
- Join loyalty programs
- Check for university food co-ops
- Follow budget food blogs

MEAL PLANNING AND PREP

Remember that time you stared into your fridge at 9 PM, hoping dinner would magically appear? Been there, done that! After a term of random panic-buying and late-night takeaways, I discovered the life-changing magic of meal planning. Here's how to get your food life together (even if the rest of your life isn't!).

The Art of Student Meal Planning

The Weekly Game Plan

Start with these power moves:

- Sunday Strategy Session
  - Check your schedule (including late lectures)
  - Plan around social events
  - Account for library study sessions
  - Factor in that inevitable hangover day
- Reality Check Planning
  - Be honest about your cooking energy
  - Include some 'lazy meals'
  - Plan for leftovers
  - Keep some emergency backup meals

The Template Method

Here's your foolproof weekly template:

- Breakfast: Rotate 2-3 easy options
- Lunch: Batch cook or prep components
- Dinner: Mix of quick and proper meals
- Snacks: Always have emergency study fuel

Batch Cooking Brilliance

The Sunday Meal Prep Party

Turn on some music and knock these out:

1. Protein Prep
- Cook a big batch of chicken
- Roast chickpeas
- Boil eggs for the week
- Prep tofu (for our veggie friends)
2. Carb Loading
- Cook rice/quinoa
- Roast sweet potatoes
- Prep pasta salad base
- Make overnight oats
3. Veggie Victory
- Chop raw veggies for snacking
- Roast vegetable medley
- Make simple salad bases
- Freeze extra portions

Storage Smarts

Because nobody wants Monday's lunch to taste funky on Thursday:

- Container Strategy

- Glass for reheating
- Plastic for freezing
- Small containers for sauces
- Jar salads for freshness
- Labelling System
  - Date everything
  - Contents (you'll forget!)
  - Reheating instructions
  - "Eat by" reminders

Time-Saving Kitchen Hacks

The Multi-Task Method

Make your kitchen time count:

- While pasta boils, prep tomorrow's lunch
- As chicken bakes, chop week's veggies
- During rice cooking, make several sauces
- Clean as you go (future-you will be grateful)

NUTRITION BASICS

Let's be real – between pulling all-nighters and surviving on coffee, student life isn't exactly known for peak nutrition. But here's the thing: your brain needs proper fuel to ace those exams, and your body needs more than just instant noodles to survive those long library sessions. Here's how to eat well without turning into a health-food influencer!

The Student Food Pyramid

Foundation Foods (Your Daily Must-Haves)

- Carbs (Yes, They're Your Friends!)
  - Brown rice/pasta (slower energy release)
  - Wholemeal bread (keeps you fuller longer)
  - Oats (breakfast champion)
  - Sweet potatoes (vitamin powerhouse)
- Proteins (Budget-Friendly Options)
  - Eggs (nature's multivitamin)
  - Lentils/beans (cheap and filling)
  - Canned tuna (emergency protein)
  - Chicken thighs (cheaper than breast, more flavor)
- Fruits & Veggies (The "Don't Skip These" Squad)
  - Frozen veg (cheaper and lasts longer)
  - Bananas (nature's energy bar)
  - Apples (perfect lecture snack)
  - Spinach (chuck it in everything)

Brain Food for Study Sessions

Because Red Bull isn't a food group:

- Pre-Study Fuel
  - Porridge with banana
  - Wholegrain toast with eggs
  - Greek yogurt with berries
  - Peanut butter sandwich
- Library Session Snacks
  - Trail mix (make your own)
  - Dark chocolate (yes, it's good for you!)
  - Fresh fruit (no sticky keyboards)
  - Cereal bars (check sugar content)

Quick Nutrition Hacks

The 'Better Than Nothing' Rules

- Something is better than nothing for breakfast
- Any vegetable is better than no vegetable
- Water first, caffeine second
- Sleep > late-night snacking

TROUBLESHOOTING AND KITCHEN HACKS

Look, we've all been there – the pasta's stuck to the pan, the rice is somehow both burnt and raw, and that sauce definitely doesn't look like the recipe picture. Don't panic! After three years of kitchen disasters (and eventual triumphs), I'm here to share every trick and fix I've learned the hard way.

Common Kitchen Catastrophes and Quick Fixes

The Burnt Pan Panic

When your pan looks like a crime scene:
- Don't Scrape! (you'll damage the pan)
- The Soda Savior:
1. Cover bottom with water
2. Add a cup of baking soda
3. Simmer for 15 minutes
4. Watch the burnt bits float away
- Vinegar Victory:
    - Equal parts water and vinegar
    - Boil for 10 minutes
    - Stuck bits will surrender

Seasoning Situations

When your taste buds are crying:
- Too Salty:
    - Add potato chunks (they absorb salt)
    - Dilute with water/stock
    - Add cream or butter
    - Serve with plain rice
- Too Spicy:
    - Dairy is your friend (yogurt/milk)
    - Add sugar or honey
    - Serve with bread/rice
    - Don't drink water (it makes it worse!)

Emergency Substitutions

The "I Forgot to Buy..." Solutions
- No Eggs?
    - Mashed banana (in baking)
    - 2 tbsp water + 1 tbsp oil
    - Greek yogurt (in most recipes)
- No Fresh Garlic?
    - Garlic powder (1/4 tsp = 1 clove)
    - Onion powder
    - Lazy garlic from a jar

Equipment Emergencies

When your kitchen tools betray you:
- No Scales?
    - 1 mug = roughly 250ml
    - 1 tablespoon = 15ml

- • Handful = about 30g
- Broken Microwave?
  - • Steam in pan with lid
  - • Use hob for reheating
  - • Make friends with neighbor

Genius Kitchen Shortcuts

Time-Saving Tricks
- Soften butter quickly: grate it!
- Peel ginger with a spoon (less waste)
- Use dental floss to cut soft cheese
- Microwave lemons for more juice

Clean-Up Hacks

- Line grill pan with foil
- Put newspaper on top of cupboards
- Keep sink caddy for sponges
- Clean microwave with lemon water

Perfect Porridge (5 Ways)

Prep: 5 mins | Cook: 5 mins | Serves: 1

Ingredients:

- US: 40g rolled oats, 250ml milk or water, pinch of salt
- UK: 40g rolled oats, 250ml milk or water, pinch of salt

Instructions:

1. In a saucepan, combine the rolled oats, milk (or water), and a pinch of salt.
2. Bring to a simmer over medium heat, stirring frequently.
3. Cook for about 5 minutes until the porridge thickens to your desired consistency.
4. Here are 5 delicious variations:
- Banana & Honey: Add sliced banana and a drizzle of honey.
- Apple & Cinnamon: Stir in grated apple and a sprinkle of cinnamon.
- Nutty Delight: Top with mixed nuts and a spoonful of nut butter.
- Berry Burst: Add fresh or frozen berries for sweetness.
- Chocolate Chip: Mix in dark chocolate chips for a treat.
5. Serve warm and enjoy your Perfect Porridge!

Nutritional Info (plain): Calories: 180 | Fat: 3g | Carbs: 30g | Protein: 7g

Note: Porridge is a versatile base—get creative with your toppings! You can also make it the night before and heat it up for a speedy breakfast.

Overnight Oats for the Organised

Prep: 5 mins | Cook: 0 mins | Serves: 1

Ingredients:

- US: 50g rolled oats, 150ml milk or almond milk, 1 tablespoon chia seeds, 1 tablespoon honey, fruit of your choice (e.g., berries or banana)
- UK: 50g rolled oats, 150ml milk or almond milk, 1 tablespoon chia seeds, 1 tablespoon honey, fruit of your choice (e.g., berries or banana)

Instructions:

1. In a jar or bowl, mix the rolled oats, milk, chia seeds, and honey until well combined.
2. Top with your choice of fruit.
3. Cover and refrigerate overnight.
4. In the morning, give it a good stir and enjoy straight from the jar or bowl!

Nutritional Info: Calories: 300 | Fat: 7g | Carbs: 45g | Protein: 10g

Note: Overnight oats last for up to 3 days in the fridge, so you can batch prep for the week. For extra creaminess, try adding a spoonful of yogurt to the mixture.

Microwave Full English

Prep: 5 mins | Cook: 10 mins | Serves: 1

Ingredients:
- US: 1 sausage, 2 eggs, 1 tomato, 2 slices of bread, 100g baked beans, salt, pepper
- UK: 1 sausage, 2 eggs, 1 tomato, 2 slices of bread, 100g baked beans, salt, pepper

Instructions:
1. Start by pricking the sausage with a fork and placing it on a microwave-safe plate. Microwave on high for 3 minutes.
2. While the sausage is cooking, cut the tomato in half and place it cut-side up on the plate. Microwave for another 2 minutes.
3. In a mug, crack in the eggs, add a pinch of salt and pepper, and whisk well. Microwave for 1 minute or until just set, stirring halfway.
4. Toast your slices of bread in a toaster.
5. Heat the baked beans in a separate bowl in the microwave for 1 minute.
6. Assemble your Full English: place the sausage, eggs, tomato, and baked beans on your plate alongside the toast. Enjoy!

Nutritional Info: Calories: 550 | Fat: 28g | Carbs: 50g | Protein: 30g

Note: This quick microwave version of the classic Full English is great for when you're short on time. Feel free to add mushrooms or swap sausage for veggie alternatives.

Power-Packed Smoothie Bowl

Prep: 5 mins | Cook: 0 mins | Serves: 1

Ingredients:
- US: 1 banana, 100g frozen berries, 150ml milk or yogurt, 30g granola, 1 tablespoon honey (optional)
- UK: 1 banana, 100g frozen berries, 150ml milk or yogurt, 30g granola, 1 tablespoon honey (optional)

Instructions:
1. In a blender, combine the banana, frozen berries, and milk (or yogurt). Blend until smooth and creamy.
2. Pour the smoothie mixture into a bowl.
3. Top with granola and a drizzle of honey if desired.
4. Feel free to add extra toppings like sliced fruits or nuts to make it even more delicious!

Nutritional Info: Calories: 350 | Fat: 5g | Carbs: 60g | Protein: 10g

Note: You can switch up the fruits or even add spinach for an extra nutrient boost. Smoothie bowls are perfect for customising to your taste.

Avocado Toast (3 Variations)

Prep: 5 mins | Cook: 0 mins | Serves: 1

Ingredients:

- US: 1 ripe avocado, 2 slices of wholemeal bread, salt, pepper
- UK: 1 ripe avocado, 2 slices of wholemeal bread, salt, pepper

Instructions:

1. Toast your slices of wholemeal bread to your preference.
2. While the bread is toasting, cut the avocado in half, remove the pit, and scoop the flesh into a bowl.
3. Mash the avocado with a fork and season with salt and pepper.
4. Spread the mashed avocado on the toasted bread.
5. Here are 3 tasty variations:
- Classic: Top with a drizzle of olive oil and a sprinkle of red pepper flakes.
- Egg-cellent: Add a poached or fried egg on top.
- Tomato Twist: Add sliced cherry tomatoes and fresh basil.

6. Enjoy your avocado toast as a trendy and satisfying breakfast!

Nutritional Info: Calories: 400 | Fat: 22g | Carbs: 36g | Protein: 10g

Note: Avocado toast is endlessly customisable—try topping it with feta, smoked salmon, or chilli flakes for extra flavour.

Breakfast Burrito

Prep: 10 mins | Cook: 10 mins | Serves: 1

Ingredients:

- US: 2 eggs, 1 tortilla, 50g cheese (grated), 50g cooked beans, 1 small avocado (sliced), salsa (optional), salt, pepper
- UK: 2 eggs, 1 tortilla, 50g cheese (grated), 50g cooked beans, 1 small avocado (sliced), salsa (optional), salt, pepper

Instructions:

1. In a bowl, crack the eggs and whisk with a pinch of salt and pepper.
2. Heat a small frying pan over medium heat. Pour in the eggs and scramble them until fully cooked (about 3-5 minutes).
3. Lay the tortilla flat on a plate and sprinkle half the cheese on one side.
4. Spoon the scrambled eggs, beans, sliced avocado, and the remaining cheese onto the tortilla. Add salsa if you like.
5. Fold in the sides of the tortilla and roll it up tightly.
6. Optional: Toast the burrito in a dry pan for 2-3 minutes on each side until golden and crispy.
7. Cut in half and dig in!

Nutritional Info: Calories: 450 | Fat: 25g | Carbs: 35g | Protein: 20g

Note: This burrito is perfect for meal prep. Wrap it in foil and save it for lunch or freeze it for later!

Veggie-Loaded Frittata

Prep: 10 mins | Cook: 20 mins | Serves: 2

Ingredients:
- US: 4 eggs, 100g mixed vegetables (like bell peppers, onions, and spinach), 50g cheese (grated), salt, pepper, olive oil
- UK: 4 eggs, 100g mixed vegetables (like bell peppers, onions, and spinach), 50g cheese (grated), salt, pepper, olive oil

Instructions:
1. Preheat your oven to 180°C (350°F).
2. In a bowl, whisk the eggs and season with salt and pepper.
3. In an oven-safe skillet, heat a splash of olive oil over medium heat. Add the mixed vegetables and sauté for about 5 minutes until tender.
4. Pour the whisked eggs over the veggies, then sprinkle the cheese on top.
5. Cook on the stove for another 5 minutes until the edges start to set, then transfer to the oven.
6. Bake for 15 minutes until the frittata is puffed up and golden.
7. Slice and serve warm for a filling meal!

Nutritional Info: Calories: 300 | Fat: 20g | Carbs: 5g | Protein: 18g

Note: Frittatas are great for using up leftover veggies. You can also add ham, bacon, or smoked salmon if you want some extra protein.

Pancakes from Scratch

Prep: 10 mins | Cook: 15 mins | Serves: 4 (makes about 8 pancakes)

Ingredients:
- US: 150g plain flour, 2 tablespoons sugar, 1 tablespoon baking powder, 1 egg, 250ml milk, 30g melted butter, a pinch of salt
- UK: 150g plain flour, 2 tablespoons sugar, 1 tablespoon baking powder, 1 egg, 250ml milk, 30g melted butter, a pinch of salt

Instructions:
1. In a large bowl, whisk together the flour, sugar, baking powder, and salt.
2. In a separate bowl, beat the egg and mix in the milk and melted butter.
3. Gradually pour the wet ingredients into the dry ingredients, whisking until smooth.
4. Heat a non-stick pan over medium heat and lightly grease with a little butter or oil.
5. Pour about 60ml (¼ cup) of batter into the pan for each pancake. Cook for 2-3 minutes until bubbles form on the surface, then flip and cook for another 2 minutes or until golden brown.
6. Serve hot with your favourite toppings such as syrup, fruit, or yogurt!

Nutritional Info (per pancake): Calories: 140 | Fat: 6g | Carbs: 18g | Protein: 4g

Note: For fluffier pancakes, try not to overmix the batter. If you're feeling fancy, throw in some chocolate chips, blueberries, or even a handful of oats for extra texture.

Greek Yogurt Parfait

Prep: 5 mins | Cook: 0 mins | Serves: 1

Ingredients:
- US: 200g Greek yogurt, 50g granola, 100g fresh berries (such as strawberries, blueberries, or raspberries), 1 tablespoon honey
- UK: 200g Greek yogurt, 50g granola, 100g fresh berries (such as strawberries, blueberries, or raspberries), 1 tablespoon honey

Instructions:
1. In a glass or bowl, spoon half of the Greek yogurt.
2. Layer half of the fresh berries over the yogurt.
3. Sprinkle half of the granola on top of the berries.
4. Repeat the layers with the remaining yogurt, berries, and granola.
5. Drizzle the honey over the top.
6. Enjoy immediately for a delicious and healthy breakfast or snack!

Nutritional Info: Calories: 300 | Fat: 8g | Carbs: 45g | Protein: 12g

Note: This parfait is highly customisable. Swap out the berries for any seasonal fruit or add a sprinkle of seeds or nuts for extra crunch. You can also use flavoured yogurt for a sweeter treat!

Breakfast Sandwich Deluxe

Prep: 5 mins | Cook: 10 mins | Serves: 1

Ingredients:
- US: 2 slices of wholemeal bread, 1 egg, 1 slice of cheese, 2 slices of cooked bacon or ham, 1 small avocado (sliced), 1 tablespoon butter, salt, pepper
- UK: 2 slices of wholemeal bread, 1 egg, 1 slice of cheese, 2 slices of cooked bacon or ham, 1 small avocado (sliced), 1 tablespoon butter, salt, pepper

Instructions:
1. Heat a small frying pan over medium heat and melt half the butter.
2. Crack the egg into the pan and fry to your preference (sunny side up or over-easy). Season with a pinch of salt and pepper. Set aside once cooked.
3. In the same pan, cook the bacon or ham slices for 2-3 minutes until warm and crispy.
4. Toast your bread slices in a toaster or under the grill until golden.
5. Butter one side of each slice of toasted bread. Place a slice of cheese on the bottom piece.
6. Layer the egg, bacon or ham, and avocado slices on top of the cheese.
7. Top with the second slice of toast, buttered side facing in.
8. Optional: Toast the entire sandwich in the frying pan for 1-2 minutes on each side to melt the cheese and crisp up the bread.
9. Slice in half and enjoy your Breakfast Sandwich Deluxe!

Nutritional Info: Calories: 450 | Fat: 25g | Carbs: 35g | Protein: 20g

Note: You can easily switch things up by adding sautéed spinach, tomatoes, or swapping ham for sausage. For a healthier option, use wholegrain bread and low-fat cheese.

Ultimate Meal Prep Salad

Prep: 15 mins | Cook: 10 mins | Serves: 4

Ingredients:
- US: 200g quinoa, 1 cucumber (diced), 1 red bell pepper (diced), 200g cherry tomatoes (halved), 1 small red onion (finely chopped), 100g feta cheese (crumbled), 50g olives (optional), 30ml olive oil, 1 tablespoon lemon juice, salt, pepper
- UK: 200g quinoa, 1 cucumber (diced), 1 red pepper (diced), 200g cherry tomatoes (halved), 1 small red onion (finely chopped), 100g feta cheese (crumbled), 50g olives (optional), 30ml olive oil, 1 tablespoon lemon juice, salt, pepper

Instructions:
1. Cook the quinoa according to the package instructions and allow it to cool completely.
2. In a large mixing bowl, combine the diced cucumber, red pepper, cherry tomatoes, red onion, and crumbled feta.
3. Once the quinoa has cooled, toss it into the vegetable mix.
4. Drizzle the olive oil and lemon juice over the salad. Season with salt and pepper.
5. Give everything a good mix and adjust seasoning to taste.
6. Divide into meal prep containers and refrigerate. It will keep fresh for 3-4 days.

Nutritional Info: Calories: 300 | Fat: 12g | Carbs: 35g | Protein: 10g

Note: Add grilled chicken or avocado for extra protein. This salad is perfect for grab-and-go lunches.

Hearty Soup in a Flask

Prep: 10 mins | Cook: 20 mins | Serves: 2

Ingredients:
- US: 1 tablespoon olive oil, 1 small onion (chopped), 1 carrot (chopped), 1 potato (diced), 1 garlic clove (minced), 400ml vegetable stock, 200g canned tomatoes, 1 teaspoon dried thyme, salt, pepper
- UK: 1 tablespoon olive oil, 1 small onion (chopped), 1 carrot (chopped), 1 potato (diced), 1 garlic clove (minced), 400ml vegetable stock, 200g tinned tomatoes, 1 teaspoon dried thyme, salt, pepper

Instructions:
1. Heat the olive oil in a pot over medium heat. Add the onion, carrot, and potato. Cook for 5-7 minutes until they begin to soften.
2. Stir in the minced garlic and cook for another minute.
3. Pour in the vegetable stock and canned tomatoes. Add the thyme and season with salt and pepper.
4. Bring the soup to a simmer and cook for 15-20 minutes until the vegetables are tender.
5. Use a hand blender to blend the soup until smooth (or leave it chunky if you prefer).
6. Pour into a thermos flask to take with you for a warming lunch on the go.

Nutritional Info: Calories: 180 | Fat: 5g | Carbs: 30g | Protein: 3g

Note: Add a dash of cream or a handful of fresh herbs to elevate the flavour. Perfect for cold days when you need something comforting.

Wraps That Won't Go Soggy

Prep: 10 mins | Cook: 0 mins | Serves: 2

Ingredients:
- US: 2 large whole wheat wraps, 100g hummus, 1 cucumber (sliced), 1 red bell pepper (sliced), 1 small carrot (grated), 100g cooked chicken or falafel, 50g baby spinach
- UK: 2 large wholemeal wraps, 100g hummus, 1 cucumber (sliced), 1 red pepper (sliced), 1 small carrot (grated), 100g cooked chicken or falafel, 50g baby spinach

Instructions:
1. Spread a generous layer of hummus across the middle of each wrap, keeping it away from the edges.
2. Layer the cucumber, pepper, carrot, and baby spinach evenly on top of the hummus.
3. Add the cooked chicken or falafel on top of the vegetables.
4. Fold in the sides of the wrap, then roll it up tightly from the bottom to the top.
5. Slice the wrap in half diagonally, wrap in foil or parchment, and store in the fridge for a quick lunch that stays fresh.

Nutritional Info: Calories: 350 | Fat: 15g | Carbs: 40g | Protein: 18g

Note: The key to avoiding soggy wraps is keeping wet ingredients like tomatoes or dressing separate until you're ready to eat.

Protein-Packed Pasta Salad

Prep: 10 mins | Cook: 10 mins | Serves: 3

Ingredients:
- US: 200g whole wheat pasta, 150g cooked chicken breast (chopped), 100g cherry tomatoes (halved), 50g spinach, 50g feta cheese (crumbled), 30ml olive oil, 1 tablespoon balsamic vinegar, salt, pepper
- UK: 200g wholemeal pasta, 150g cooked chicken breast (chopped), 100g cherry tomatoes (halved), 50g spinach, 50g feta cheese (crumbled), 30ml olive oil, 1 tablespoon balsamic vinegar, salt, pepper

Instructions:
1. Cook the pasta according to package instructions, then drain and allow to cool.
2. In a large bowl, combine the cooked pasta, chopped chicken, cherry tomatoes, spinach, and crumbled feta.
3. Drizzle the olive oil and balsamic vinegar over the salad and toss everything together.
4. Season with salt and pepper to taste.
5. Divide into containers and refrigerate for up to 3 days.

Nutritional Info: Calories: 400 | Fat: 18g | Carbs: 40g | Protein: 25g

Note: This pasta salad is perfect for meal prepping—add a handful of nuts or seeds for an extra crunch.

Stuffed Pitta Pockets

Prep: 10 mins | Cook: 0 mins | Serves: 2

Ingredients:

- US: 2 whole wheat pitta breads, 100g cooked chicken or falafel, 50g mixed salad greens, 50g cucumber (sliced), 50g cherry tomatoes (halved), 2 tablespoons hummus
- UK: 2 wholemeal pitta breads, 100g cooked chicken or falafel, 50g mixed salad greens, 50g cucumber (sliced), 50g cherry tomatoes (halved), 2 tablespoons hummus

Instructions:

1. Warm the pitta breads in the toaster or under the grill for 1-2 minutes until soft.
2. Cut each pitta in half to create pockets.
3. Spread a tablespoon of hummus inside each pitta pocket.
4. Stuff the pitta with the mixed greens, cucumber, cherry tomatoes, and chicken or falafel.
5. Enjoy immediately or wrap in foil for lunch on the go.

Nutritional Info: Calories: 350 | Fat: 10g | Carbs: 45g | Protein: 18g

Note: Pitta pockets are great for packing up lunch. Swap hummus for tzatziki or add sliced avocado for extra creaminess.

Bento Box Lunch

Prep: 15 mins | Cook: 0 mins | Serves: 1

Ingredients:

- US: 50g cooked chicken breast or tofu, 50g cooked quinoa or rice, 50g sliced cucumber, 50g cherry tomatoes, 1 boiled egg, 1 tablespoon soy sauce (for dipping)
- UK: 50g cooked chicken breast or tofu, 50g cooked quinoa or rice, 50g sliced cucumber, 50g cherry tomatoes, 1 boiled egg, 1 tablespoon soy sauce (for dipping)

Instructions:

1. Cook your quinoa or rice according to package instructions. Allow it to cool.
2. In your bento box, arrange the cooked chicken or tofu, quinoa or rice, sliced cucumber, cherry tomatoes, and a boiled egg.
3. Place a small container of soy sauce for dipping in the box.
4. Secure the lid and refrigerate until ready to eat.

Nutritional Info: Calories: 350 | Fat: 15g | Carbs: 35g | Protein: 25g

Note: Feel free to swap the ingredients based on your preferences. This is a versatile lunch option that's both healthy and satisfying.

Homemade Pot Noodle

Prep: 5 mins | Cook: 5 mins | Serves: 1

Ingredients:

- US: 1 packet instant noodles, 50g frozen peas, 50g cooked chicken or tofu (chopped), 1 tablespoon soy sauce, 1 spring onion (chopped), 1 teaspoon sesame oil
- UK: 1 packet instant noodles, 50g frozen peas, 50g cooked chicken or tofu (chopped), 1 tablespoon soy sauce, 1 spring onion (chopped), 1 teaspoon sesame oil

Instructions:

1. Cook the instant noodles according to the packet instructions. Drain and set aside.
2. In a small pot, heat the frozen peas in boiling water for 2 minutes until soft. Drain.
3. In a jar or pot, layer the noodles, peas, cooked chicken or tofu, and spring onion.
4. Drizzle with soy sauce and sesame oil.
5. When ready to eat, add boiling water to the jar and let it sit for a few minutes. Stir and enjoy your homemade pot noodle!

Nutritional Info: Calories: 350 | Fat: 10g | Carbs: 50g | Protein: 15g

Vegetarian Sushi Rolls

Prep: 20 mins | Cook: 0 mins | Serves: 2

Ingredients:
- US: 200g sushi rice, 300ml water, 4 nori sheets, 1 avocado (sliced), 1 cucumber (julienned), 1 carrot (julienned), soy sauce (for dipping)
- UK: 200g sushi rice, 300ml water, 4 nori sheets, 1 avocado (sliced), 1 cucumber (julienned), 1 carrot (julienned), soy sauce (for dipping)

Instructions:
1. Rinse the sushi rice under cold water until the water runs clear. Combine with water in a pot and bring to a boil. Reduce heat, cover, and simmer for 15 minutes. Let it cool.
2. Place a nori sheet on a bamboo sushi mat (or a clean kitchen towel).
3. Spread a thin layer of sushi rice on the nori, leaving a 2cm border at the top.
4. Lay slices of avocado, cucumber, and carrot along the bottom edge of the rice.
5. Roll the mat away from you, pressing gently to form a tight roll. Seal the edge with a little water.
6. Slice into bite-sized pieces and serve with soy sauce.

Nutritional Info: Calories: 250 | Fat: 10g | Carbs: 35g | Protein: 6g

Note: Get creative with fillings! You can use any veggies or add cooked shrimp or crab for a non-vegetarian version.

Chickpea and Tuna Salad

Prep: 10 mins | Cook: 0 mins | Serves: 2

Ingredients:
- US: 200g canned chickpeas (drained), 150g canned tuna (drained), 50g red onion (finely chopped), 50g cherry tomatoes (halved), 30ml olive oil, 1 tablespoon lemon juice, salt, pepper
- UK: 200g canned chickpeas (drained), 150g canned tuna (drained), 50g red onion (finely chopped), 50g cherry tomatoes (halved), 30ml olive oil, 1 tablespoon lemon juice, salt, pepper

Instructions:
1. In a large mixing bowl, combine the chickpeas, tuna, red onion, and cherry tomatoes.
2. Drizzle with olive oil and lemon juice. Season with salt and pepper to taste.
3. Toss everything together until well combined.
4. Serve immediately or store in the fridge for up to 2 days.

Nutritional Info: Calories: 350 | Fat: 15g | Carbs: 30g | Protein: 25g

Note: This salad is high in protein and perfect for a quick lunch. You can also add chopped herbs like parsley or coriander for extra flavour.

Microwave Jacket Potato with Toppings

Prep: 5 mins | Cook: 10 mins | Serves: 1

Ingredients:
- US: 1 large potato, 50g grated cheese, 100g baked beans, 1 tablespoon sour cream, salt, pepper
- UK: 1 large potato, 50g grated cheese, 100g baked beans, 1 tablespoon sour cream, salt, pepper

Instructions:
1. Wash the potato thoroughly and prick it several times with a fork.
2. Place the potato on a microwave-safe plate and microwave on high for 8-10 minutes, turning halfway, until soft.
3. Carefully slice the potato open and fluff the insides with a fork.
4. Top with grated cheese, baked beans, sour cream, and season with salt and pepper.
5. Serve hot and enjoy your delicious, quick meal!

Nutritional Info: Calories: 400 | Fat: 15g | Carbs: 55g | Protein: 12g

Note: You can add any toppings you like—try coleslaw, tuna, or even leftover chili for a filling meal!

One-Pot Spaghetti Bolognese

Prep: 10 mins | Cook: 30 mins | Serves: 4

Ingredients:
- US: 500g ground beef, 1 onion (chopped), 2 garlic cloves (minced), 400g canned tomatoes, 200g tomato sauce, 250g spaghetti, 1 tablespoon olive oil, 500ml beef broth, 1 teaspoon dried oregano, salt, pepper, grated parmesan (optional)
- UK: 500g minced beef, 1 onion (chopped), 2 garlic cloves (minced), 400g tinned tomatoes, 200g tomato passata, 250g spaghetti, 1 tablespoon olive oil, 500ml beef stock, 1 teaspoon dried oregano, salt, pepper, grated parmesan (optional)

Instructions:
1. Heat the olive oil in a large pot over medium heat. Add the chopped onion and garlic, and cook for 2-3 minutes until softened.
2. Add the minced beef, breaking it up with a wooden spoon, and cook until browned.
3. Pour in the canned tomatoes, tomato sauce, and beef broth. Stir in the oregano, and season with salt and pepper.
4. Break the spaghetti in half and add it directly into the pot, making sure it's submerged in the liquid.
5. Bring the mixture to a simmer, cover, and cook for 15 minutes, stirring occasionally to prevent the pasta from sticking.
6. Once the pasta is tender and the sauce has thickened, serve with grated parmesan on top.

Nutritional Info: Calories: 500 | Fat: 18g | Carbs: 60g | Protein: 30g

Note: This recipe makes cleanup easy by cooking everything in one pot. For a vegetarian version, swap beef for lentils or soy mince.

Chickpea and Spinach Curry

Prep: 10 mins | Cook: 20 mins | Serves: 4

Ingredients:
- US: 1 tablespoon olive oil, 1 onion (chopped), 2 garlic cloves (minced), 1 tablespoon curry powder, 400g canned chickpeas (drained), 400g canned tomatoes, 200g fresh spinach, 100ml coconut milk, salt, pepper
- UK: 1 tablespoon olive oil, 1 onion (chopped), 2 garlic cloves (minced), 1 tablespoon curry powder, 400g tinned chickpeas (drained), 400g tinned tomatoes, 200g fresh spinach, 100ml coconut milk, salt, pepper

Instructions:
1. Heat the olive oil in a large pan over medium heat. Add the chopped onion and garlic, and sauté for 3-4 minutes until softened.
2. Stir in the curry powder and cook for another minute to release the flavours.
3. Add the chickpeas and tinned tomatoes, and bring to a simmer.
4. Stir in the fresh spinach and cook until wilted.
5. Pour in the coconut milk and simmer for 5 more minutes, allowing the curry to thicken.
6. Season with salt and pepper to taste, and serve over rice or with naan bread.

Nutritional Info: Calories: 320 | Fat: 12g | Carbs: 40g | Protein: 10g

Note: You can make this curry spicier by adding a pinch of chilli flakes. It's perfect for batch cooking and freezes well.

Easy Chicken Stir Fry

Prep: 10 mins | Cook: 15 mins | Serves: 2

Ingredients:

- US: 2 chicken breasts (sliced), 1 red bell pepper (sliced), 1 carrot (julienned), 100g broccoli, 2 tablespoons soy sauce, 1 tablespoon oyster sauce, 1 tablespoon olive oil, 1 garlic clove (minced), 1 teaspoon sesame oil, rice (for serving)
- UK: 2 chicken breasts (sliced), 1 red pepper (sliced), 1 carrot (julienned), 100g broccoli, 2 tablespoons soy sauce, 1 tablespoon oyster sauce, 1 tablespoon olive oil, 1 garlic clove (minced), 1 teaspoon sesame oil, rice (for serving)

Instructions:

1. Heat the olive oil in a wok or large frying pan over medium heat.
2. Add the sliced chicken and cook for 5-6 minutes until golden and fully cooked through.
3. Add the minced garlic, red pepper, carrot, and broccoli to the pan. Stir fry for 5 minutes until the vegetables are tender-crisp.
4. Pour in the soy sauce and oyster sauce, and stir everything together.
5. Drizzle with sesame oil for extra flavour, and serve over rice.

Nutritional Info: Calories: 400 | Fat: 15g | Carbs: 40g | Protein: 35g

Note: Use pre-cut stir fry vegetables to save time. This meal is great for a quick, healthy dinner after a long day.

Vegetarian Chilli

Prep: 10 mins | Cook: 25 mins | Serves: 4

Ingredients:

- US: 1 tablespoon olive oil, 1 onion (chopped), 2 garlic cloves (minced), 1 red bell pepper (chopped), 400g canned kidney beans (drained), 400g canned black beans (drained), 400g canned tomatoes, 2 teaspoons chilli powder, 1 teaspoon cumin, salt, pepper
- UK: 1 tablespoon olive oil, 1 onion (chopped), 2 garlic cloves (minced), 1 red pepper (chopped), 400g tinned kidney beans (drained), 400g tinned black beans (drained), 400g tinned tomatoes, 2 teaspoons chilli powder, 1 teaspoon cumin, salt, pepper

Instructions:

1. Heat the olive oil in a large pot over medium heat. Add the onion, garlic, and red pepper, and sauté for 5 minutes until softened.
2. Stir in the chilli powder and cumin, and cook for another minute.
3. Add the kidney beans, black beans, and tinned tomatoes. Bring to a simmer.
4. Cover and cook for 20 minutes, stirring occasionally, until the chilli has thickened.
5. Season with salt and pepper to taste, and serve with rice, tortilla chips, or on its own.

Nutritional Info: Calories: 250 | Fat: 6g | Carbs: 40g | Protein: 12g

Note: You can top the chilli with sour cream, grated cheese, or avocado for extra richness.

Foolproof Risotto

Prep: 10 mins | Cook: 25 mins | Serves: 4

Ingredients:
- US: 300g arborio rice, 1 onion (chopped), 2 garlic cloves (minced), 1 litre chicken or vegetable broth, 100ml white wine (optional), 50g grated parmesan, 1 tablespoon olive oil, 100g mushrooms (optional), salt, pepper
- UK: 300g arborio rice, 1 onion (chopped), 2 garlic cloves (minced), 1 litre chicken or vegetable stock, 100ml white wine (optional), 50g grated parmesan, 1 tablespoon olive oil, 100g mushrooms (optional), salt, pepper

Instructions:
1. Heat the olive oil in a large pan over medium heat. Add the onion and garlic, and cook for 5 minutes until softened.
2. Stir in the arborio rice and cook for 2 minutes until the edges of the rice are translucent.
3. Add the white wine (if using) and stir until absorbed.
4. Gradually add the broth, one ladleful at a time, stirring frequently, until the liquid is absorbed and the rice is creamy and tender (about 20 minutes).
5. Stir in the parmesan, season with salt and pepper, and serve immediately.

Nutritional Info: Calories: 400 | Fat: 12g | Carbs: 60g | Protein: 10g

Note: Add mushrooms, peas, or even prawns for extra flavour. Risotto is a great way to impress without too much effort!

Baked Salmon with Roasted Veg

Prep: 10 mins | Cook: 20 mins | Serves: 2

Ingredients:
- US: 2 salmon fillets, 1 tablespoon olive oil, 200g baby potatoes (halved), 1 red bell pepper (sliced), 1 courgette (sliced), 1 teaspoon dried thyme, salt, pepper, lemon wedges (for serving)
- UK: 2 salmon fillets, 1 tablespoon olive oil, 200g baby potatoes (halved), 1 red pepper (sliced), 1 courgette (sliced), 1 teaspoon dried thyme, salt, pepper, lemon wedges (for serving)

Instructions:
1. Preheat the oven to 200°C (400°F).
2. Toss the potatoes, red pepper, and courgette with olive oil, thyme, salt, and pepper. Spread them out on a baking tray.
3. Roast the vegetables for 15 minutes.
4. After 15 minutes, place the salmon fillets on the tray, skin-side down, and roast for an additional 10 minutes, or until the salmon is cooked through.
5. Serve with lemon wedges for a fresh, zesty finish.

Nutritional Info: Calories: 450 | Fat: 25g | Carbs: 30g | Protein: 30g

Note: Swap the salmon for chicken breasts if you prefer, adjusting the cooking time as needed.

Homemade Pizza

Prep: 10 mins | Cook: 20 mins | Serves: 2 personal pizzas

Ingredients:
- US: 250g plain flour, 7g instant yeast, 150ml warm water, 1 tablespoon olive oil, 100g pizza sauce, 150g shredded mozzarella, 50g pepperoni (optional), 1 teaspoon dried oregano, salt
- UK: 250g plain flour, 7g instant yeast, 150ml warm water, 1 tablespoon olive oil, 100g pizza sauce, 150g grated mozzarella, 50g pepperoni (optional), 1 teaspoon dried oregano, salt

Instructions:
1. Preheat your oven to 220°C (425°F).
2. In a large bowl, mix the flour, yeast, and a pinch of salt. Gradually add the warm water and olive oil, stirring until it forms a dough.
3. Knead the dough on a floured surface for 5 minutes until smooth.
4. Roll out the dough into two small pizza bases and place them on a lightly oiled baking sheet.
5. Spread the pizza sauce over the bases, then sprinkle the mozzarella evenly on top. Add the pepperoni if using.
6. Bake for 10-15 minutes until the crust is golden and the cheese is melted.
7. Sprinkle with oregano before serving.

Nutritional Info: Calories: 500 | Fat: 20g | Carbs: 60g | Protein: 20g

Note: You can customise the toppings with anything you like—try mushrooms, peppers, or even pineapple for a personal touch!

Veggie-Loaded Mac and Cheese

Prep: 10 mins | Cook: 20 mins | Serves: 4

Ingredients:
- US: 300g macaroni pasta, 250g cheddar cheese (grated), 300ml milk, 30g butter, 30g flour, 1 tablespoon olive oil, 1 courgette (grated), 1 carrot (grated), salt, pepper
- UK: 300g macaroni pasta, 250g cheddar cheese (grated), 300ml milk, 30g butter, 30g flour, 1 tablespoon olive oil, 1 courgette (grated), 1 carrot (grated), salt, pepper

Instructions:
1. Cook the macaroni in a pot of boiling salted water according to the packet instructions, then drain.
2. In another pan, melt the butter over medium heat. Stir in the flour to make a roux, cooking for 1 minute.
3. Gradually whisk in the milk, stirring constantly until the sauce thickens.
4. Stir in the grated cheese until melted and smooth, then season with salt and pepper.
5. In a separate pan, heat the olive oil and sauté the grated courgette and carrot for 3-4 minutes.
6. Stir the sautéed veggies into the cheese sauce, then combine with the cooked macaroni.
7. Serve hot, and enjoy this nutritious twist on a classic!

Nutritional Info: Calories: 450 | Fat: 22g | Carbs: 45g | Protein: 18g

Note: You can bake this mac and cheese for an extra crispy topping by sprinkling some breadcrumbs on top and popping it in the oven for 10 minutes.

Teriyaki Tofu Bowl

Prep: 10 mins | Cook: 20 mins | Serves: 2

Ingredients:
- US: 200g firm tofu (cubed), 2 tablespoons soy sauce, 1 tablespoon honey, 1 tablespoon rice vinegar, 1 teaspoon sesame oil, 100g rice, 1 carrot (julienned), 100g broccoli (chopped), 1 tablespoon olive oil, sesame seeds (for garnish)
- UK: 200g firm tofu (cubed), 2 tablespoons soy sauce, 1 tablespoon honey, 1 tablespoon rice vinegar, 1 teaspoon sesame oil, 100g rice, 1 carrot (julienned), 100g broccoli (chopped), 1 tablespoon olive oil, sesame seeds (for garnish)

Instructions:
1. Cook the rice according to the package instructions.
2. In a small bowl, whisk together the soy sauce, honey, rice vinegar, and sesame oil to make the teriyaki sauce.
3. Heat the olive oil in a pan over medium heat. Add the cubed tofu and cook for 5-6 minutes until golden on all sides.
4. Add the chopped broccoli and carrot to the pan, and cook for another 3-4 minutes until the vegetables are tender.
5. Pour the teriyaki sauce over the tofu and vegetables, tossing to coat everything evenly.
6. Serve the tofu and vegetables over the rice, and garnish with sesame seeds.

Nutritional Info: Calories: 350 | Fat: 14g | Carbs: 40g | Protein: 15g

Note: Swap the tofu for chicken or beef if you prefer, and add more veggies like bell peppers or spinach for extra nutrition.

Shepherd's Pie (with Veggie Option)

Prep: 15 mins | Cook: 30 mins | Serves: 4

Ingredients:
- US: 500g ground lamb (or veggie mince), 1 onion (chopped), 2 carrots (chopped), 2 tablespoons tomato paste, 400ml beef or vegetable broth, 1 tablespoon olive oil, 1 teaspoon Worcestershire sauce, 800g potatoes (peeled and chopped), 50g butter, 50ml milk, salt, pepper
- UK: 500g minced lamb (or veggie mince), 1 onion (chopped), 2 carrots (chopped), 2 tablespoons tomato purée, 400ml beef or vegetable stock, 1 tablespoon olive oil, 1 teaspoon Worcestershire sauce, 800g potatoes (peeled and chopped), 50g butter, 50ml milk, salt, pepper

Instructions:
1. Boil the potatoes in salted water for 10-15 minutes until tender. Drain and mash with butter, milk, salt, and pepper. Set aside.
2. While the potatoes are cooking, heat the olive oil in a large pan over medium heat. Add the chopped onion and carrots, and cook for 5 minutes until softened.
3. Add the minced lamb (or veggie mince) to the pan, breaking it up and cooking until browned (about 5-7 minutes).
4. Stir in the tomato paste and Worcestershire sauce, then pour in the broth. Simmer for 10 minutes, allowing the mixture to thicken.
5. Transfer the mince mixture to an ovenproof dish and top with the mashed potatoes.
6. Place under a hot grill (broiler) for 5 minutes, or until the top is golden brown.
7. Serve hot, and enjoy this comforting classic.

Nutritional Info: Calories: 450 | Fat: 20g | Carbs: 50g | Protein: 18g

Note: You can add peas or corn to the filling for extra veg. The veggie mince version is just as hearty and flavourful!

Crispy Oven-Baked Chicken Wings

Prep: 10 mins | Cook: 35 mins | Serves: 4

Ingredients:
- US: 800g chicken wings, 1 tablespoon baking powder, 1 teaspoon garlic powder, 1 teaspoon paprika, 1 teaspoon salt, ½ teaspoon pepper, 2 tablespoons olive oil, 2 tablespoons hot sauce (optional)
- UK: 800g chicken wings, 1 tablespoon baking powder, 1 teaspoon garlic powder, 1 teaspoon paprika, 1 teaspoon salt, ½ teaspoon pepper, 2 tablespoons olive oil, 2 tablespoons hot sauce (optional)

Instructions:
1. Preheat your oven to 220°C (425°F) and line a baking tray with parchment paper.
2. In a large bowl, mix the baking powder, garlic powder, paprika, salt, and pepper.
3. Pat the chicken wings dry with kitchen paper, then toss them in the seasoning mixture until well coated.
4. Spread the wings out on the prepared baking tray, ensuring they're in a single layer. Drizzle with olive oil.
5. Bake for 30-35 minutes, flipping halfway through, until the wings are crispy and golden brown.
6. Toss in hot sauce if you want some heat, or enjoy them as they are!

Nutritional Info: Calories: 300 | Fat: 20g | Carbs: 1g | Protein: 25g

Note: The baking powder helps the wings crisp up without the need for frying. Perfect for a healthier fakeaway!

Homemade Burger and Chips

Prep: 10 mins | Cook: 30 mins | Serves: 2

Ingredients:
- US: 300g minced beef, 1 teaspoon Worcestershire sauce, 1 teaspoon garlic powder, 1 teaspoon salt, ½ teaspoon pepper, 2 burger buns, 2 slices cheddar cheese, 2 potatoes (sliced into chips), 2 tablespoons olive oil
- UK: 300g minced beef, 1 teaspoon Worcestershire sauce, 1 teaspoon garlic powder, 1 teaspoon salt, ½ teaspoon pepper, 2 burger buns, 2 slices cheddar cheese, 2 potatoes (sliced into chips), 2 tablespoons olive oil

Instructions:
1. Preheat the oven to 200°C (400°F). Toss the potato chips in olive oil and season with salt and pepper. Spread them on a baking tray and bake for 25-30 minutes, flipping halfway.
2. In a bowl, mix the minced beef with Worcestershire sauce, garlic powder, salt, and pepper. Form into two burger patties.
3. Heat a frying pan over medium heat and cook the burgers for 4-5 minutes per side, or until they're cooked to your liking.
4. Place a slice of cheese on each patty in the last minute of cooking so it melts.
5. Toast the burger buns in the same pan for a minute, then assemble your burgers with any extra toppings you like (lettuce, tomato, pickles).
6. Serve with your homemade chips for a perfect takeaway-style meal!

Nutritional Info: Calories: 650 | Fat: 35g | Carbs: 60g | Protein: 35g

Note: For a veggie option, swap the beef for a plant-based patty or a portobello mushroom.

Veggie-Packed Fried Rice

Prep: 10 mins | Cook: 10 mins | Serves: 2

Ingredients:
- US: 200g cooked rice (preferably cold), 1 carrot (chopped), 100g peas, 1 bell pepper (chopped), 2 eggs, 2 tablespoons soy sauce, 1 tablespoon sesame oil, 2 spring onions (chopped)
- UK: 200g cooked rice (preferably cold), 1 carrot (chopped), 100g peas, 1 bell pepper (chopped), 2 eggs, 2 tablespoons soy sauce, 1 tablespoon sesame oil, 2 spring onions (chopped)

Instructions:
1. Heat a tablespoon of sesame oil in a large frying pan or wok over medium heat.
2. Add the chopped carrot, peas, and bell pepper to the pan. Stir-fry for 3-4 minutes until softened.
3. Push the veggies to one side of the pan and crack the eggs into the other side. Scramble the eggs until fully cooked, then mix them with the veggies.
4. Add the cold rice to the pan, breaking up any clumps, and stir everything together.
5. Drizzle with soy sauce and stir-fry for another 3-4 minutes until the rice is heated through.
6. Garnish with chopped spring onions before serving.

Nutritional Info: Calories: 350 | Fat: 12g | Carbs: 45g | Protein: 10g

Note: Cold rice works best for fried rice to avoid it becoming mushy, so this is a great way to use up leftovers!

Easy Chicken Tikka Masala

Prep: 10 mins | Cook: 25 mins | Serves: 2

Ingredients:
- US: 300g chicken breast (diced), 2 tablespoons tikka curry paste, 200g tinned tomatoes, 100ml coconut milk, 1 onion (chopped), 1 tablespoon olive oil, 2 tablespoons plain yoghurt, rice (to serve)
- UK: 300g chicken breast (diced), 2 tablespoons tikka curry paste, 200g tinned tomatoes, 100ml coconut milk, 1 onion (chopped), 1 tablespoon olive oil, 2 tablespoons plain yoghurt, rice (to serve)

Instructions:
1. Heat olive oil in a large pan over medium heat. Add the chopped onion and cook for 3-4 minutes until softened.
2. Stir in the tikka curry paste and cook for 1 minute until fragrant.
3. Add the diced chicken and cook for 5-7 minutes until browned on all sides.
4. Pour in the tinned tomatoes and coconut milk, stirring well. Simmer for 10-15 minutes until the sauce thickens and the chicken is cooked through.
5. Stir in the plain yoghurt just before serving to make it creamy.
6. Serve with rice for a delicious fakeaway treat!

Nutritional Info: Calories: 450 | Fat: 20g | Carbs: 40g | Protein: 30g

Note: You can use leftover chicken or even chickpeas for a veggie-friendly version!

Falafel Wraps with Homemade Hummus

Prep: 15 mins | Cook: 10 mins | Serves: 4 wraps

Ingredients:
- US: 400g canned chickpeas, 1 garlic clove (minced), 2 tablespoons tahini, 1 tablespoon lemon juice, 1 tablespoon olive oil, 1 teaspoon cumin, 200g falafel, 4 wraps, lettuce, cucumber, tomatoes
- UK: 400g canned chickpeas, 1 garlic clove (minced), 2 tablespoons tahini, 1 tablespoon lemon juice, 1 tablespoon olive oil, 1 teaspoon cumin, 200g falafel, 4 wraps, lettuce, cucumber, tomatoes

Instructions:
1. To make the hummus, blend the chickpeas, garlic, tahini, lemon juice, olive oil, and cumin in a food processor until smooth. Add a splash of water if it's too thick.
2. Warm the falafel in the oven or a frying pan according to the package instructions.
3. Lay the wraps flat and spread a generous amount of hummus in the centre of each.
4. Add the lettuce, cucumber, and tomatoes on top, then place the falafel.
5. Roll up the wraps tightly and serve!

Nutritional Info: Calories: 400 | Fat: 18g | Carbs: 50g | Protein: 12g

Note: If you don't have a blender, mash the chickpeas with a fork for a chunkier hummus.

Fish and Chips in the Oven

Prep: 15 mins | Cook: 25 mins | Serves: 2

Ingredients:
- US: 400g frozen fish fillets (battered), 400g frozen chips, 1 lemon (wedges for serving), salt, and pepper
- UK: 400g frozen fish fillets (battered), 400g frozen chips, 1 lemon (wedges for serving), salt, and pepper

Instructions:
1. Preheat your oven according to the instructions on the fish and chips packaging (usually around 200°C/400°F).
2. Spread the frozen chips on a baking tray and bake as per the packet instructions (usually about 20-25 minutes).
3. Add the fish fillets to the tray for the last 10-15 minutes of cooking, or until both the fish and chips are golden and crispy.
4. Season with salt and pepper to taste, and serve with lemon wedges on the side.

Nutritional Info: Calories: 500 | Fat: 25g | Carbs: 60g | Protein: 20g

Note: Baking is a healthier alternative to frying, and it keeps the fish crispy without the hassle!

Vegetable Pad Thai

Prep: 15 mins | Cook: 10 mins | Serves: 2

Ingredients:
- US: 200g rice noodles, 100g mixed vegetables (e.g., bell peppers, carrots, beansprouts), 2 tablespoons soy sauce, 1 tablespoon peanut butter, 1 tablespoon lime juice, 1 tablespoon sugar, chopped peanuts (for garnish), lime wedges (for serving)
- UK: 200g rice noodles, 100g mixed vegetables (e.g., bell peppers, carrots, beansprouts), 2 tablespoons soy sauce, 1 tablespoon peanut butter, 1 tablespoon lime juice, 1 tablespoon sugar, chopped peanuts (for garnish), lime wedges (for serving)

Instructions:
1. Cook the rice noodles according to the packet instructions, then drain and set aside.
2. In a large frying pan, stir-fry the mixed vegetables over medium heat for about 3-4 minutes.
3. Add the cooked noodles to the pan along with the soy sauce, peanut butter, lime juice, and sugar. Stir everything together and cook for another 2-3 minutes.
4. Serve garnished with chopped peanuts and lime wedges on the side.

Nutritional Info: Calories: 400 | Fat: 15g | Carbs: 60g | Protein: 12g

Note: You can easily add tofu or chicken for extra protein if desired!

Homemade Naan Bread

Prep: 10 mins | Cook: 10 mins | Serves: 4

Ingredients:
- US: 250g plain flour, 1 teaspoon yeast, ½ teaspoon salt, 1 tablespoon sugar, 150ml warm water, 2 tablespoons yogurt, 1 tablespoon olive oil, garlic (optional, for topping)
- UK: 250g plain flour, 1 teaspoon yeast, ½ teaspoon salt, 1 tablespoon sugar, 150ml warm water, 2 tablespoons yogurt, 1 tablespoon olive oil, garlic (optional, for topping)

Instructions:
1. In a bowl, mix the flour, yeast, salt, and sugar.
2. Make a well in the centre and add the warm water, yogurt, and olive oil. Mix until a dough forms.
3. Knead the dough for about 5 minutes until smooth, then cover and let it rise in a warm place for 30 minutes.
4. Preheat a frying pan over medium heat.
5. Divide the dough into 4 pieces and roll each out into an oval shape. Cook each naan in the frying pan for 2-3 minutes on each side until golden and puffy.
6. Optional: Rub with garlic or butter before serving.

Nutritional Info: Calories: 250 | Fat: 7g | Carbs: 40g | Protein: 8g

Note: These naan breads are perfect for dipping in your favourite curries or serving with hummus!

Sweet and Sour Tofu

Prep: 15 mins | Cook: 15 mins | Serves: 2

Ingredients:

- US: 300g firm tofu (cubed), 1 bell pepper (chopped), 1 onion (sliced), 100g pineapple chunks, 2 tablespoons sweet and sour sauce, 1 tablespoon soy sauce, 1 tablespoon cornflour, 2 tablespoons vegetable oil
- UK: 300g firm tofu (cubed), 1 bell pepper (chopped), 1 onion (sliced), 100g pineapple chunks, 2 tablespoons sweet and sour sauce, 1 tablespoon soy sauce, 1 tablespoon cornflour, 2 tablespoons vegetable oil

Instructions:

1. Pat the tofu dry with kitchen paper and toss it in cornflour until well coated.
2. Heat vegetable oil in a frying pan over medium heat. Add the tofu and cook for about 5-7 minutes until golden brown.
3. Add the onion and bell pepper to the pan and stir-fry for another 3-4 minutes.
4. Stir in the pineapple chunks, sweet and sour sauce, and soy sauce. Cook for an additional 2-3 minutes until everything is heated through.
5. Serve hot over rice or noodles for a delightful fakeaway!

Nutritional Info: Calories: 400 | Fat: 20g | Carbs: 40g | Protein: 20g

Note: This dish is great for using up leftover vegetables, so feel free to add any you have on hand!

Loaded Nachos Supreme

Prep: 10 mins | Cook: 10 mins | Serves: 2

Ingredients:

- US: 200g tortilla chips, 100g grated cheese (cheddar or Monterey Jack), 100g canned black beans (drained), 100g salsa, 1 jalapeño (sliced), 2 tablespoons sour cream, chopped fresh coriander (for garnish)
- UK: 200g tortilla chips, 100g grated cheese (cheddar or Monterey Jack), 100g canned black beans (drained), 100g salsa, 1 jalapeño (sliced), 2 tablespoons sour cream, chopped fresh coriander (for garnish)

Instructions:

1. Preheat your oven to 200°C (400°F).
2. On a large baking tray, spread the tortilla chips evenly.
3. Sprinkle the grated cheese over the chips, followed by the black beans and jalapeño slices.
4. Bake in the oven for 5-7 minutes, or until the cheese is melted and bubbling.
5. Remove from the oven and drizzle with salsa and sour cream.
6. Garnish with fresh coriander and enjoy your nachos straight away!

Nutritional Info: Calories: 600 | Fat: 30g | Carbs: 65g | Protein: 15g

Note: Feel free to add any extra toppings you love, like guacamole or diced tomatoes!

Garlic and Herb Butter Steak

Prep: 10 mins | Cook: 15 mins | Serves: 2

Ingredients:
- US: 2 ribeye steaks (about 250g each), 30g unsalted butter, 3 cloves garlic (minced), 1 tablespoon fresh rosemary (chopped), 1 tablespoon fresh thyme (chopped), salt, and pepper
- UK: 2 ribeye steaks (about 250g each), 30g unsalted butter, 3 cloves garlic (minced), 1 tablespoon fresh rosemary (chopped), 1 tablespoon fresh thyme (chopped), salt, and pepper

Instructions:
1. Take the steaks out of the fridge and let them come to room temperature for about 15 minutes.
2. Season both sides of the steaks generously with salt and pepper.
3. In a frying pan, melt the butter over medium heat. Add the minced garlic, rosemary, and thyme.
4. When the butter is bubbling, add the steaks. Cook for about 4-5 minutes on each side for medium-rare, basting them with the garlic herb butter.
5. Remove the steaks from the pan and let them rest for 5 minutes before slicing.
6. Serve the steaks drizzled with the garlic and herb butter from the pan.

Nutritional Info: Calories: 500 | Fat: 40g | Carbs: 0g | Protein: 40g

Note: Pair with a simple side salad or roasted vegetables for a complete meal!

Creamy Mushroom Pasta

Prep: 10 mins | Cook: 15 mins | Serves: 2

Ingredients:
- US: 200g pasta (e.g., fettuccine), 150g mushrooms (sliced), 1 clove garlic (minced), 100ml cream, 30g parmesan cheese (grated), 1 tablespoon olive oil, salt, and pepper
- UK: 200g pasta (e.g., fettuccine), 150g mushrooms (sliced), 1 clove garlic (minced), 100ml cream, 30g parmesan cheese (grated), 1 tablespoon olive oil, salt, and pepper

Instructions:
1. Cook the pasta according to the packet instructions. Reserve a cup of pasta water and drain the rest.
2. In a large frying pan, heat the olive oil over medium heat and sauté the garlic and mushrooms for about 5 minutes until softened.
3. Pour in the cream and stir in the parmesan cheese. Cook for another 2-3 minutes, adding reserved pasta water until you reach your desired consistency.
4. Toss the cooked pasta in the creamy sauce. Season with salt and pepper.
5. Serve hot, garnished with extra parmesan if desired.

Nutritional Info: Calories: 600 | Fat: 25g | Carbs: 80g | Protein: 15g

Note: You can add spinach or chicken for extra nutrition and flavor!

Stuffed Bell Peppers

Prep: 15 mins | Cook: 30 mins | Serves: 2

Ingredients:
- US: 2 bell peppers (halved and cored), 200g cooked rice, 150g minced beef (or lentils for vegetarian), 1 can (400g) diced tomatoes, 1 teaspoon paprika, 30g cheese (grated), salt, and pepper
- UK: 2 bell peppers (halved and cored), 200g cooked rice, 150g minced beef (or lentils for vegetarian), 1 can (400g) diced tomatoes, 1 teaspoon paprika, 30g cheese (grated), salt, and pepper

Instructions:
1. Preheat your oven to 180°C (350°F).
2. In a frying pan, brown the minced beef (or lentils) over medium heat. Stir in the diced tomatoes, cooked rice, paprika, salt, and pepper. Cook for about 5 minutes.
3. Spoon the mixture into the halved bell peppers and place them in a baking dish.
4. Top each pepper with grated cheese.
5. Bake for 25-30 minutes until the peppers are tender and the cheese is melted and bubbly.
6. Serve hot with a side salad.

Nutritional Info: Calories: 450 | Fat: 15g | Carbs: 50g | Protein: 25g

Note: Feel free to customize the stuffing with whatever ingredients you have on hand!

Homemade Gnocchi with Sage Butter

Prep: 20 mins | Cook: 15 mins | Serves: 2

Ingredients:
- US: 300g potatoes (peeled and cubed), 100g flour, 1 egg, 30g butter, 6 sage leaves, salt
- UK: 300g potatoes (peeled and cubed), 100g flour, 1 egg, 30g butter, 6 sage leaves, salt

Instructions:
1. Boil the potatoes in salted water until tender, then drain and mash them.
2. Allow the mash to cool, then mix in the flour and egg until a dough forms.
3. On a floured surface, roll out the dough and cut it into small pieces. Shape each piece into a gnocchi.
4. In a large pot of salted boiling water, cook the gnocchi until they float (about 2-3 minutes).
5. In a frying pan, melt the butter and add the sage leaves, cooking until fragrant.
6. Toss the cooked gnocchi in the sage butter and serve hot.

Nutritional Info: Calories: 400 | Fat: 18g | Carbs: 55g | Protein: 10g

Note: Serve with grated parmesan for added flavor!

Baked Cod with Lemon and Herbs

Prep: 10 mins | Cook: 20 mins | Serves: 2

Ingredients:
- US: 2 cod fillets (about 200g each), 1 lemon (sliced), 30ml olive oil, 1 teaspoon dried thyme, salt, and pepper
- UK: 2 cod fillets (about 200g each), 1 lemon (sliced), 30ml olive oil, 1 teaspoon dried thyme, salt, and pepper

Instructions:
1. Preheat your oven to 200°C (400°F).
2. Place the cod fillets in a baking dish and drizzle with olive oil.
3. Sprinkle with thyme, salt, and pepper, then top with lemon slices.
4. Bake for 15-20 minutes until the fish is cooked through and flakes easily with a fork.
5. Serve with steamed vegetables or rice.

Nutritional Info: Calories: 300 | Fat: 15g | Carbs: 2g | Protein: 35g

Note: You can use any white fish for this recipe!

Vegetarian Lasagna

Prep: 20 mins | Cook: 40 mins | Serves: 4

Ingredients:

- US: 9 lasagna sheets, 300g spinach, 200g ricotta cheese, 200g mozzarella cheese (grated), 500g passata, 1 onion (chopped), 2 cloves garlic (minced), 1 tablespoon olive oil, salt, and pepper
- UK: 9 lasagna sheets, 300g spinach, 200g ricotta cheese, 200g mozzarella cheese (grated), 500g passata, 1 onion (chopped), 2 cloves garlic (minced), 1 tablespoon olive oil, salt, and pepper

Instructions:

1. Preheat your oven to 180°C (350°F).
2. In a frying pan, heat olive oil over medium heat. Add the onion and garlic, cooking until softened. Stir in the spinach until wilted, then remove from heat.
3. In a baking dish, spread a layer of passata, then place three lasagna sheets on top.
4. Layer with half the ricotta, half the spinach mixture, and a third of the mozzarella. Repeat the layers, finishing with a layer of passata and remaining mozzarella.
5. Bake for 30-40 minutes until golden and bubbling.
6. Serve hot, garnished with fresh basil if desired.

Nutritional Info: Calories: 350 | Fat: 15g | Carbs: 40g | Protein: 18g

Note: This lasagna can be made ahead of time and stored in the fridge before baking!

Roasted Vegetable Tart

Prep: 15 mins | Cook: 30 mins | Serves: 4

Ingredients:

- US: 1 sheet puff pastry, 200g mixed vegetables (e.g., zucchini, bell peppers, onions), 100g feta cheese, 1 egg, 30ml cream, salt, and pepper
- UK: 1 sheet puff pastry, 200g mixed vegetables (e.g., zucchini, bell peppers, onions), 100g feta cheese, 1 egg, 30ml cream, salt, and pepper

Instructions:

1. Preheat your oven to 200°C (400°F).
2. Roll out the puff pastry onto a baking tray lined with parchment paper.
3. In a bowl, whisk the egg and cream together, then spread it over the pastry, leaving a border.
4. Arrange the mixed vegetables on top and crumble feta cheese over everything.
5. Season with salt and pepper, then bake for 25-30 minutes until golden brown.
6. Serve warm or at room temperature.

Nutritional Info: Calories: 300 | Fat: 20g | Carbs: 25g | Protein: 10g

Note: You can use any vegetables you like for this tart!

Prawn and Chorizo Paella

Prep: 15 mins | Cook: 30 mins | Serves: 2

Ingredients:
- US: 150g arborio rice, 200g prawns (peeled), 100g chorizo (sliced), 400ml chicken stock, 1 bell pepper (chopped), 1 onion (chopped), 2 cloves garlic (minced), 1 teaspoon paprika, 1 tablespoon olive oil
- UK: 150g arborio rice, 200g prawns (peeled), 100g chorizo (sliced), 400ml chicken stock, 1 bell pepper (chopped), 1 onion (chopped), 2 cloves garlic (minced), 1 teaspoon paprika, 1 tablespoon olive oil

Instructions:
1. In a large frying pan, heat olive oil over medium heat and cook the chorizo until browned.
2. Add the onion, garlic, and bell pepper, cooking for another 5 minutes.
3. Stir in the rice and paprika, then pour in the chicken stock.
4. Bring to a simmer and cook for about 15 minutes, adding the prawns in the last 5 minutes.
5. Once the rice is tender and the liquid is absorbed, serve hot.

Nutritional Info: Calories: 500 | Fat: 20g | Carbs: 50g | Protein: 30g

Stuffed Chicken Breast

Prep: 15 mins | Cook: 30 mins | Serves: 2

Ingredients:
- US: 2 chicken breasts, 100g spinach, 50g cream cheese, 50g mozzarella cheese (grated), 1 tablespoon olive oil, salt, and pepper
- UK: 2 chicken breasts, 100g spinach, 50g cream cheese, 50g mozzarella cheese (grated), 1 tablespoon olive oil, salt, and pepper

Instructions:
1. Preheat your oven to 200°C (400°F).
2. In a frying pan, sauté the spinach in olive oil until wilted. Mix with cream cheese and mozzarella.
3. Cut a pocket in each chicken breast and stuff with the spinach mixture.
4. Season the outside of the chicken with salt and pepper, then place in a baking dish.
5. Bake for 25-30 minutes until the chicken is cooked through.
6. Serve with a side of vegetables or salad.

Nutritional Info: Calories: 450 | Fat: 20g | Carbs: 4g | Protein: 50g

Lentil and Mushroom Wellington

Prep: 20 mins | Cook: 30 mins | Serves: 4

Ingredients:
- US: 1 sheet puff pastry, 200g lentils (cooked), 150g mushrooms (chopped), 1 onion (chopped), 2 cloves garlic (minced), 1 egg (for egg wash), 1 tablespoon olive oil, salt, and pepper
- UK: 1 sheet puff pastry, 200g lentils (cooked), 150g mushrooms (chopped), 1 onion (chopped), 2 cloves garlic (minced), 1 egg (for egg wash), 1 tablespoon olive oil, salt, and pepper

Instructions:
1. Preheat your oven to 200°C (400°F).
2. In a frying pan, heat olive oil and sauté the onion and garlic until softened. Add the mushrooms and cook until browned.
3. Stir in the cooked lentils and season with salt and pepper. Remove from heat and let it cool.
4. Roll out the puff pastry and place the lentil mixture in the centre. Fold the pastry over to seal it.
5. Brush with beaten egg and place on a baking tray. Bake for 25-30 minutes until golden brown.
6. Serve hot, sliced into portions.

Nutritional Info: Calories: 400 | Fat: 25g | Carbs: 35g | Protein: 15g

Note: This vegetarian dish is hearty and perfect for impressing your date!

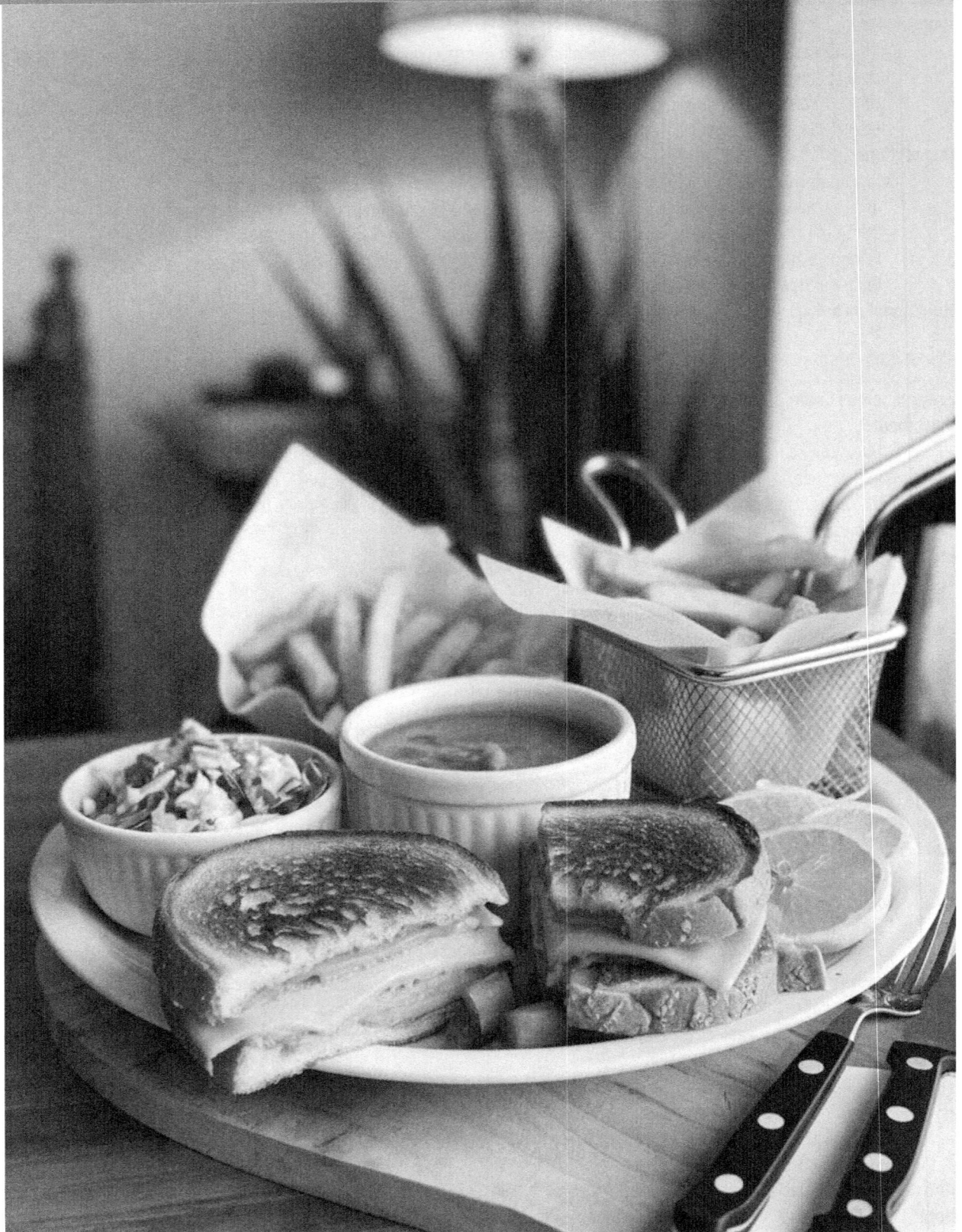

Crispy Garlic Roast Potatoes

Prep: 10 mins | Cook: 45 mins | Serves: 4

Ingredients:
- US: 1kg potatoes (peeled and chopped), 4 cloves garlic (minced), 30ml olive oil, 1 teaspoon dried thyme, salt, and pepper
- UK: 1kg potatoes (peeled and chopped), 4 cloves garlic (minced), 30ml olive oil, 1 teaspoon dried thyme, salt, and pepper

Instructions:
1. Preheat your oven to 200°C (400°F).
2. Toss the potatoes with olive oil, minced garlic, thyme, salt, and pepper in a large bowl.
3. Spread the potatoes in a single layer on a baking tray.
4. Roast for 35-45 minutes, turning halfway through, until golden and crispy.
5. Serve hot and crispy as a perfect side dish for any meal.

Nutritional Info: Calories: 250 | Fat: 8g | Carbs: 38g | Protein: 4g

Note: You can use any type of potato for this recipe!

Homemade Hummus (3 Flavours)

Prep: 10 mins | Cook: 0 mins | Serves: 4

Ingredients (Base):
- US: 400g canned chickpeas (drained), 60ml tahini, 2 tablespoons lemon juice, 2 tablespoons olive oil, 2 cloves garlic, salt
- UK: 400g canned chickpeas (drained), 60ml tahini, 2 tablespoons lemon juice, 2 tablespoons olive oil, 2 cloves garlic, salt

For Flavours:
- Classic: Use the base recipe as is.
- Red Pepper: Add 1 roasted red pepper.
- Spicy: Add 1 teaspoon of cayenne pepper and 1 tablespoon hot sauce.

Instructions:
1. In a food processor, combine chickpeas, tahini, lemon juice, olive oil, garlic, and salt. Blitz until smooth.
2. For red pepper hummus, add the roasted pepper and blend. For spicy hummus, add cayenne and hot sauce.
3. Adjust seasoning to taste.
4. Serve with pita bread or veggie sticks.

Nutritional Info (per serving): Calories: 180 | Fat: 10g | Carbs: 16g | Protein: 5g

Note: Store leftovers in the fridge for up to 3 days!

Loaded Sweet Potato Fries

Prep: 10 mins | Cook: 30 mins | Serves: 4

Ingredients:
- US: 3 medium sweet potatoes (cut into fries), 30ml olive oil, 50g cheddar cheese (grated), 2 tablespoons sour cream, 1 tablespoon chives (chopped), salt, and pepper
- UK: 3 medium sweet potatoes (cut into fries), 30ml olive oil, 50g cheddar cheese (grated), 2 tablespoons sour cream, 1 tablespoon chives (chopped), salt, and pepper

Instructions:
1. Preheat your oven to 220°C (425°F).
2. Toss the sweet potato fries with olive oil, salt, and pepper. Spread on a baking tray.
3. Bake for 25-30 minutes, turning halfway through, until crispy.
4. Remove from the oven, sprinkle with grated cheese, and return to the oven for 2-3 minutes until melted.
5. Serve with sour cream and a sprinkle of chopped chives.

Nutritional Info: Calories: 320 | Fat: 15g | Carbs: 38g | Protein: 7g

Note: These fries make a great snack or a light meal!

Cheesy Garlic Bread

Prep: 5 mins | Cook: 10 mins | Serves: 4

Ingredients:
- US: 1 baguette (sliced), 50g butter (softened), 3 cloves garlic (minced), 100g mozzarella cheese (grated), 1 tablespoon parsley (chopped)
- UK: 1 baguette (sliced), 50g butter (softened), 3 cloves garlic (minced), 100g mozzarella cheese (grated), 1 tablespoon parsley (chopped)

Instructions:
1. Preheat your oven to 180°C (350°F).
2. In a bowl, mix the butter, garlic, and parsley. Spread over the slices of baguette.
3. Sprinkle grated mozzarella over each slice.
4. Place the baguette on a baking tray and bake for 8-10 minutes until golden and the cheese is melted.
5. Serve hot with your favourite pasta dish or as a snack.

Nutritional Info: Calories: 320 | Fat: 15g | Carbs: 40g | Protein: 10g

Note: You can also make this with vegan cheese and butter for a dairy-free version!

Spicy Roasted Chickpeas

Prep: 5 mins | Cook: 30 mins | Serves: 4

Ingredients:
- US: 400g canned chickpeas (drained), 15ml olive oil, 1 teaspoon paprika, 1 teaspoon cumin, 1/2 teaspoon cayenne pepper, salt
- UK: 400g canned chickpeas (drained), 15ml olive oil, 1 teaspoon paprika, 1 teaspoon cumin, 1/2 teaspoon cayenne pepper, salt

Instructions:
1. Preheat your oven to 200°C (400°F).
2. Toss the chickpeas with olive oil, paprika, cumin, cayenne, and salt until evenly coated.
3. Spread the chickpeas on a baking tray in a single layer.
4. Roast for 25-30 minutes, shaking the tray halfway through, until crispy and golden.
5. Allow to cool before serving.

Nutritional Info: Calories: 140 | Fat: 5g | Carbs: 20g | Protein: 5g

Note: These make a great healthy snack or salad topper!

Homemade Guacamole

Prep: 10 mins | Cook: 0 mins | Serves: 4

Ingredients:
- US: 2 ripe avocados, 1 small tomato (diced), 1/2 red onion (finely chopped), 1 tablespoon lime juice, 1 tablespoon coriander (chopped), salt, and pepper
- UK: 2 ripe avocados, 1 small tomato (diced), 1/2 red onion (finely chopped), 1 tablespoon lime juice, 1 tablespoon coriander (chopped), salt, and pepper

Instructions:
1. In a bowl, mash the avocados with a fork.
2. Stir in the diced tomato, red onion, lime juice, and coriander.
3. Season with salt and pepper to taste.
4. Serve immediately with tortilla chips or veggie sticks.

Nutritional Info: Calories: 180 | Fat: 15g | Carbs: 10g | Protein: 2g

Note: For extra spice, add chopped jalapeños!

Veggie Crudités with Dips

Prep: 10 mins | Cook: 0 mins | Serves: 4

Ingredients:
- US: 2 carrots (cut into sticks), 1 cucumber (cut into sticks), 1 bell pepper (sliced), 100g cherry tomatoes, 100g hummus, 100g tzatziki
- UK: 2 carrots (cut into sticks), 1 cucumber (cut into sticks), 1 bell pepper (sliced), 100g cherry tomatoes, 100g hummus, 100g tzatziki

Instructions:
1. Arrange the carrot sticks, cucumber, bell pepper slices, and cherry tomatoes on a platter.
2. Serve with small bowls of hummus and tzatziki for dipping.
3. Enjoy as a healthy snack or starter.

Nutritional Info: Calories: 150 | Fat: 7g | Carbs: 15g | Protein: 4g

Note: You can mix and match the veggies depending on what you have!

Cheesy Nachos

Prep: 5 mins | Cook: 10 mins | Serves: 4

Ingredients:
- US: 200g tortilla chips, 150g cheddar cheese (grated), 50g jalapeños (sliced), 2 tablespoons sour cream, 2 tablespoons salsa
- UK: 200g tortilla chips, 150g cheddar cheese (grated), 50g jalapeños (sliced), 2 tablespoons sour cream, 2 tablespoons salsa

Instructions:
1. Preheat your oven to 180°C (350°F).
2. Spread the tortilla chips in a single layer on a baking tray.
3. Sprinkle the grated cheese and jalapeños over the top.
4. Bake for 8-10 minutes until the cheese is melted.
5. Serve with sour cream and salsa on the side for dipping.

Nutritional Info: Calories: 350 | Fat: 20g | Carbs: 30g | Protein: 10g

Note: Add guacamole for extra flavour!

Stuffed Mushrooms

Prep: 10 mins | Cook: 20 mins | Serves: 4

Ingredients:
- US: 8 large mushrooms, 100g cream cheese, 50g cheddar cheese (grated), 2 cloves garlic (minced), 1 tablespoon parsley (chopped), salt, and pepper
- UK: 8 large mushrooms, 100g cream cheese, 50g cheddar cheese (grated), 2 cloves garlic (minced), 1 tablespoon parsley (chopped), salt, and pepper

Instructions:
1. Preheat your oven to 180°C (350°F).
2. Remove the mushroom stems and finely chop them.
3. In a bowl, mix the chopped stems with cream cheese, cheddar, garlic, parsley, salt, and pepper.
4. Stuff the mushroom caps with the mixture and place on a baking tray.
5. Bake for 15-20 minutes until golden and bubbling.
6. Serve as a snack or side dish.

Nutritional Info: Calories: 150 | Fat: 10g | Carbs: 5g | Protein: 6g

Note: You can also add bacon bits for a meatier version!

Homemade Popcorn (3 Ways)

Prep: 5 mins | Cook: 5 mins | Serves: 4

Ingredients:
- US: 100g popcorn kernels, 2 tablespoons oil
- UK: 100g popcorn kernels, 2 tablespoons oil

For Flavours:
- Sweet: 2 tablespoons sugar, 1 teaspoon cinnamon
- Savoury: 1 tablespoon butter, 1 teaspoon salt
- Spicy: 1 teaspoon paprika, 1 teaspoon chilli powder

Instructions:
1. Heat oil in a large pot over medium heat.
2. Add popcorn kernels and cover with a lid. Shake occasionally until popping slows down.
3. Remove from heat and transfer to a bowl.
4. For sweet popcorn, toss with sugar and cinnamon. For savoury, drizzle with melted butter and sprinkle with salt. For spicy, toss with paprika and chilli powder.

Nutritional Info (per serving): Calories: 120 | Fat: 5g | Carbs: 15g | Protein: 3g

Note: Experiment with your favourite seasonings!

Slow Cooker Pulled Pork

Prep: 10 mins | Cook: 8 hours | Serves: 6

Ingredients:
- US: 1.5kg pork shoulder, 120ml BBQ sauce, 60ml apple cider vinegar, 1 tablespoon paprika, 1 tablespoon brown sugar, 1 teaspoon garlic powder, salt, and pepper
- UK: 1.5kg pork shoulder, 120ml BBQ sauce, 60ml apple cider vinegar, 1 tablespoon paprika, 1 tablespoon brown sugar, 1 teaspoon garlic powder, salt, and pepper

Instructions:
1. Rub the pork shoulder with paprika, brown sugar, garlic powder, salt, and pepper.
2. Place the pork in your slow cooker and pour in the BBQ sauce and apple cider vinegar.
3. Cover and cook on low for 8 hours or on high for 4-5 hours, until the pork is tender and easy to shred.
4. Remove the pork from the slow cooker, shred it using two forks, and stir it back into the sauce.
5. Serve in soft rolls, tacos, or over rice, and enjoy a week of easy pulled pork meals!

Nutritional Info: Calories: 350 | Fat: 15g | Carbs: 10g | Protein: 40g

Veggie-Loaded Frittata Muffins

Prep: 10 mins | Cook: 20 mins | Serves: 12 muffins

Ingredients:
- US: 8 eggs, 100g spinach (chopped), 1 bell pepper (diced), 50g cheddar cheese (grated), 1 tablespoon olive oil, salt, and pepper
- UK: 8 eggs, 100g spinach (chopped), 1 bell pepper (diced), 50g cheddar cheese (grated), 1 tablespoon olive oil, salt, and pepper

Instructions:
1. Preheat your oven to 180°C (350°F) and grease a muffin tin with olive oil.
2. In a bowl, whisk together the eggs and season with salt and pepper.
3. Stir in the spinach, diced bell pepper, and cheddar cheese.
4. Pour the mixture evenly into the muffin cups.
5. Bake for 18-20 minutes, or until the frittatas are set and golden on top.
6. Let them cool before storing in the fridge for an easy grab-and-go breakfast!

Nutritional Info: Calories: 90 | Fat: 6g | Carbs: 1g | Protein: 7g

Freezer-Friendly Burritos

Prep: 15 mins | Cook: 10 mins | Serves: 6 burritos

Ingredients:
- US: 6 large tortillas, 400g black beans (drained), 200g cooked rice, 100g cheddar cheese (grated), 1 bell pepper (diced), 100g salsa, 2 tablespoons sour cream, salt, and pepper
- UK: 6 large tortillas, 400g black beans (drained), 200g cooked rice, 100g cheddar cheese (grated), 1 bell pepper (diced), 100g salsa, 2 tablespoons sour cream, salt, and pepper

Instructions:
1. Lay out the tortillas and divide the rice, black beans, diced bell pepper, and grated cheese evenly between them.
2. Add a spoonful of salsa and sour cream to each tortilla, then season with salt and pepper.
3. Roll up the burritos tightly, tucking in the sides as you go.
4. Wrap each burrito in foil and store in the freezer.
5. To reheat, remove the foil and microwave on high for 2-3 minutes, or until heated through.

Nutritional Info: Calories: 350 | Fat: 12g | Carbs: 45g | Protein: 14g

Mason Jar Salads

Prep: 15 mins | Cook: 0 mins | Serves: 4 jars

Ingredients:
- US: 4 large mason jars, 200g cooked quinoa, 100g cherry tomatoes (halved), 100g cucumber (diced), 100g feta cheese (crumbled), 50g spinach, 4 tablespoons vinaigrette
- UK: 4 large mason jars, 200g cooked quinoa, 100g cherry tomatoes (halved), 100g cucumber (diced), 100g feta cheese (crumbled), 50g spinach, 4 tablespoons vinaigrette

Instructions:
1. In each mason jar, layer the ingredients starting with the vinaigrette at the bottom.
2. Add the quinoa next, followed by the cherry tomatoes, cucumber, feta cheese, and spinach on top.
3. Seal the jars tightly and store them in the fridge for up to 4 days.
4. When ready to eat, just shake the jar to mix everything together!

Nutritional Info: Calories: 300 | Fat: 15g | Carbs: 30g | Protein: 10g

Note: Switch up the veggies and proteins for different flavour combos.

Bulk-Cooked Shredded Chicken

Prep: 10 mins | Cook: 30 mins | Serves: 8 portions

Ingredients:
- US: 1.2kg chicken breasts, 500ml chicken broth, 1 teaspoon garlic powder, 1 teaspoon paprika, salt, and pepper
- UK: 1.2kg chicken breasts, 500ml chicken broth, 1 teaspoon garlic powder, 1 teaspoon paprika, salt, and pepper

Instructions:
1. Place the chicken breasts in a large pot and cover with chicken broth.
2. Add garlic powder, paprika, salt, and pepper.
3. Bring to a simmer over medium heat, then reduce the heat to low and cook for 25-30 minutes, or until the chicken is fully cooked.
4. Remove the chicken from the pot and shred using two forks.
5. Store in portions in the fridge or freezer for quick meals like tacos, salads, or sandwiches!

Nutritional Info: Calories: 150 | Fat: 3g | Carbs: 0g | Protein: 30g

Note: Keeps in the fridge for 3-4 days or in the freezer for up to 3 months.

Breakfast Sandwiches for the Week

Prep: 15 mins | Cook: 10 mins | Serves: 6 sandwiches

Ingredients:
- US: 6 English muffins, 6 eggs, 6 slices cheddar cheese, 6 slices ham or bacon, 1 tablespoon butter, salt, and pepper
- UK: 6 English muffins, 6 eggs, 6 slices cheddar cheese, 6 slices ham or bacon, 1 tablespoon butter, salt, and pepper

Instructions:
1. Preheat your oven to 180°C (350°F) and toast the English muffins.
2. Fry the eggs in butter, seasoning with salt and pepper.
3. Assemble each sandwich with an egg, slice of cheese, and ham or bacon.
4. Wrap each sandwich in foil and freeze.
5. Reheat in the microwave for 1-2 minutes for a quick, filling breakfast!

Nutritional Info: Calories: 350 | Fat: 18g | Carbs: 30g | Protein: 15g

Note: Switch out the ham for a veggie option if preferred!

Marinated Tofu Cubes

Prep: 10 mins | Cook: 20 mins | Serves: 4

Ingredients:
- US:400g firm tofu, 60ml soy sauce, 30ml sesame oil, 1 tablespoon rice vinegar, 1 teaspoon ginger (grated), 1 teaspoon garlic (minced)
- UK: 400g firm tofu, 60ml soy sauce, 30ml sesame oil, 1 tablespoon rice vinegar, 1 teaspoon ginger (grated), 1 teaspoon garlic (minced)

Instructions:
1. Press the tofu to remove excess moisture, then cut it into cubes.
2. In a bowl, whisk together the soy sauce, sesame oil, rice vinegar, ginger, and garlic.
3. Marinate the tofu in this mixture for at least 15 minutes.
4. Heat a non-stick skillet over medium heat and cook the tofu for 10-15 minutes until golden.
5. Serve it over rice or in stir-fries!

Nutritional Info: Calories: 150 | Fat: 9g | Carbs: 6g | Protein: 12g

Note: Tofu is great for protein-packed meals!

Homemade Granola Bars

Prep: 10 mins | Cook: 20 mins | Serves: 12 bars
Ingredients:
- US: 250g oats, 100g honey, 50g peanut butter, 100g mixed nuts (chopped), 50g dried fruit, 1 teaspoon vanilla extract
- UK: 250g oats, 100g honey, 50g peanut butter, 100g mixed nuts (chopped), 50g dried fruit, 1 teaspoon vanilla extract

Instructions:
1. Preheat your oven to 180°C (350°F) and line a baking dish with parchment paper.
2. In a saucepan, melt honey and peanut butter over low heat, stirring until combined.
3. In a bowl, mix oats, chopped nuts, dried fruit, and vanilla extract.
4. Pour the melted mixture over the dry ingredients and mix well.
5. Press the mixture into the baking dish and bake for 15-20 minutes.
6. Let cool, then cut into bars and enjoy!

Nutritional Info: Calories: 180 | Fat: 8g | Carbs: 25g | Protein: 5g
Note: These are perfect for a quick breakfast or a post-workout snack!

Energy Balls (3 Flavours)

Prep: 10 mins | Cook: 0 mins | Serves: 12 balls
Ingredients:
- US: 200g oats, 100g peanut butter, 50g honey, 50g chocolate chips (for chocolate flavour), 50g dried fruit (for fruity flavour), 50g cocoa powder (for chocolate flavour)
- UK: 200g oats, 100g peanut butter, 50g honey, 50g chocolate chips (for chocolate flavour), 50g dried fruit (for fruity flavour), 50g cocoa powder (for chocolate flavour)

Instructions:
1. In a bowl, mix oats, peanut butter, honey, and your choice of flavourings.
2. Roll the mixture into small balls and place them on a tray.
3. Refrigerate for 30 minutes to firm up.
4. Store in an airtight container in the fridge for easy snacks!

Nutritional Info: Calories: 120 | Fat: 5g | Carbs: 15g | Protein: 4g
Note: Customize with your favourite nuts or seeds!

Vegetarian Chilli

Prep: 10 mins | Cook: 40 mins | Serves: 6
Ingredients:
- US: 1 tablespoon olive oil, 1 onion (diced), 2 cloves garlic (minced), 1 bell pepper (diced), 400g canned kidney beans (drained), 400g canned tomatoes, 1 teaspoon chilli powder, 1 teaspoon cumin, salt, and pepper
- UK: 1 tablespoon olive oil, 1 onion (diced), 2 cloves garlic (minced), 1 bell pepper (diced), 400g canned kidney beans (drained), 400g canned tomatoes, 1 teaspoon chilli powder, 1 teaspoon cumin, salt, and pepper

Instructions:
1. Heat the olive oil in a large pot over medium heat.
2. Add the diced onion, garlic, and bell pepper and sauté for 5-7 minutes until soft.
3. Stir in the kidney beans, canned tomatoes, chilli powder, cumin, salt, and pepper.
4. Bring to a simmer and cook for 30 minutes, stirring occasionally.
5. Serve with rice or tortilla chips, and garnish with sour cream or cheese.

Nutritional Info: Calories: 250 | Fat: 5g | Carbs: 40g | Protein: 10g
Note: Great for freezing and reheating later!

Full English Breakfast Wrap

Prep: 10 mins | Cook: 15 mins | Serves: 2 wraps

Ingredients:
- US: 4 large eggs, 4 slices bacon, 2 sausages, 2 large tortillas, 100g baked beans, 50g mushrooms (sliced), 30ml olive oil, salt, and pepper
- UK: 4 large eggs, 4 slices bacon, 2 sausages, 2 large tortillas, 100g baked beans, 50g mushrooms (sliced), 30ml olive oil, salt, and pepper

Instructions:
1. In a frying pan, heat the olive oil over medium heat and cook the bacon until crispy. Remove and set aside.
2. In the same pan, cook the sausages according to package instructions, then add the mushrooms and cook until soft.
3. In a bowl, beat the eggs with salt and pepper, then pour them into the pan, scrambling until fully cooked.
4. Warm the tortillas in a separate pan or microwave for a few seconds.
5. To assemble, layer the scrambled eggs, bacon, sausages, mushrooms, and baked beans in each tortilla.
6. Roll them up tightly, and enjoy your Full English Breakfast Wrap!

Nutritional Info: Calories: 600 | Fat: 35g | Carbs: 40g | Protein: 25g

Note: Perfect for a hearty breakfast that keeps you going!

Loaded Cheesy Chips

Prep: 5 mins | Cook: 15 mins | Serves: 2

Ingredients:
- US: 200g frozen chips, 100g cheddar cheese (grated), 50g jalapeños (sliced), 30ml sour cream, 2 tablespoons green onions (chopped), salt, and pepper
- UK: 200g frozen chips, 100g cheddar cheese (grated), 50g jalapeños (sliced), 30ml sour cream, 2 tablespoons spring onions (chopped), salt, and pepper

Instructions:
1. Preheat your oven and cook the frozen chips according to package instructions.
2. Once the chips are golden and crispy, remove them from the oven and sprinkle with grated cheese and jalapeños.
3. Return to the oven for an additional 5 minutes or until the cheese is melted and bubbly.
4. Drizzle with sour cream and top with chopped green onions before serving.
5. Dig in and enjoy your Loaded Cheesy Chips while they're hot!

Nutritional Info: Calories: 450 | Fat: 25g | Carbs: 35g | Protein: 15g

Note: Add your favourite toppings for a personal touch!

Breakfast Pizza

Prep: 10 mins | Cook: 15 mins | Serves: 2 pizzas

Ingredients:
- US: 1 pre-made pizza base, 4 large eggs, 100g mozzarella cheese (grated), 50g cherry tomatoes (halved), 2 tablespoons pesto, salt, and pepper
- UK: 1 pre-made pizza base, 4 large eggs, 100g mozzarella cheese (grated), 50g cherry tomatoes (halved), 2 tablespoons pesto, salt, and pepper

Instructions:
1. Preheat your oven according to the pizza base instructions.
2. Spread pesto evenly over the pizza base.
3. Scatter the mozzarella cheese and cherry tomatoes on top.
4. Crack the eggs gently onto the pizza, spacing them out evenly.
5. Bake in the oven for about 12-15 minutes, or until the eggs are set to your liking.
6. Remove from the oven, season with salt and pepper, and slice up your Breakfast Pizza!

Nutritional Info: Calories: 500 | Fat: 25g | Carbs: 45g | Protein: 20g

Note: You can add bacon or spinach for extra flavour!

Peanut Butter and Banana Smoothie

Prep: 5 mins | Cook: 0 mins | Serves: 1

Ingredients:
- US: 1 ripe banana, 200ml milk (or plant-based milk), 2 tablespoons peanut butter, 1 tablespoon honey, ice cubes (optional)
- UK: 1 ripe banana, 200ml milk (or plant-based milk), 2 tablespoons peanut butter, 1 tablespoon honey, ice cubes (optional)

Instructions:
1. In a blender, combine the banana, milk, peanut butter, honey, and ice cubes if desired.
2. Blend until smooth and creamy.
3. Pour into a glass and enjoy your delicious Peanut Butter and Banana Smoothie!

Nutritional Info: Calories: 350 | Fat: 15g | Carbs: 40g | Protein: 10g

Note: Great for a quick breakfast or snack!

Spicy Ramen Upgrade

Prep: 5 mins | Cook: 10 mins | Serves: 1

Ingredients:
- US: 1 pack instant ramen noodles, 500ml water, 1 egg, 50g spinach, 50g sliced mushrooms, 1 teaspoon sriracha, 1 green onion (chopped)
- UK: 1 pack instant ramen noodles, 500ml water, 1 egg, 50g spinach, 50g sliced mushrooms, 1 teaspoon sriracha, 1 spring onion (chopped)

Instructions:
1. In a pot, bring the water to a boil and add the ramen noodles.
2. Cook for about 3 minutes, then add the mushrooms and spinach.
3. Crack an egg directly into the pot and stir gently to poach it.
4. Once everything is cooked, stir in the sriracha and top with chopped green onion.
5. Serve hot and enjoy your Spicy Ramen Upgrade!

Nutritional Info: Calories: 350 | Fat: 15g | Carbs: 45g | Protein: 15g

Note: Adjust the spiciness to your taste!

Bacon and Egg Sandwich Deluxe

Prep: 5 mins | Cook: 10 mins | Serves: 2

Ingredients:
- US: 4 slices bread, 4 slices bacon, 2 large eggs, 50g cheddar cheese (sliced), 30g butter, salt, and pepper
- UK: 4 slices bread, 4 slices bacon, 2 large eggs, 50g cheddar cheese (sliced), 30g butter, salt, and pepper

Instructions:
1. In a frying pan, cook the bacon until crispy. Remove and drain on paper towels.
2. In the same pan, use the bacon fat to fry the eggs, seasoning with salt and pepper.
3. Toast the bread slices and spread butter on one side of each.
4. Assemble the sandwich: place a slice of cheese, a fried egg, and two slices of bacon on one slice of buttered bread. Top with another slice and grill on a pan until golden.
5. Cut in half and enjoy your Bacon and Egg Sandwich Deluxe!

Nutritional Info: Calories: 500 | Fat: 35g | Carbs: 30g | Protein: 20g

Note: Add avocado for a creamy twist!

Homemade Bloody Mary (Virgin Option)

Prep: 5 mins | Cook: 0 mins | Serves: 1

Ingredients:
- US: 150ml tomato juice, 30ml lemon juice, 1 teaspoon Worcestershire sauce, 1 teaspoon hot sauce, salt, and pepper, celery stick (for garnish)
- UK: 150ml tomato juice, 30ml lemon juice, 1 teaspoon Worcestershire sauce, 1 teaspoon hot sauce, salt, and pepper, celery stick (for garnish)

Instructions:
1. In a glass, mix the tomato juice, lemon juice, Worcestershire sauce, and hot sauce.
2. Season with salt and pepper to taste, stirring well.
3. Garnish with a celery stick and enjoy your refreshing Virgin Bloody Mary!

Nutritional Info: Calories: 50 | Fat: 0g | Carbs: 10g | Protein: 2g

Note: Add olives or pickles for an extra punch!

Hangover Hash

Prep: 10 mins | Cook: 20 mins | Serves: 2

Ingredients:
- US: 400g potatoes (diced), 100g bell peppers (diced), 1 onion (diced), 4 large eggs, 30ml olive oil, salt, and pepper
- UK: 400g potatoes (diced), 100g bell peppers (diced), 1 onion (diced), 4 large eggs, 30ml olive oil, salt, and pepper

Instructions:
1. In a frying pan, heat the olive oil and add the diced potatoes. Cook for about 10 minutes until golden and crispy.
2. Add the bell peppers and onion, cooking for another 5-7 minutes until soft.
3. Make four small wells in the mixture and crack an egg into each. Cover and cook until the eggs are set to your liking.
4. Season with salt and pepper and serve hot!

Nutritional Info: Calories: 450 | Fat: 20g | Carbs: 40g | Protein: 15g

Note: This is a great way to use up leftover veggies!

Comforting Tomato Soup with Grilled Cheese

Prep: 5 mins | Cook: 15 mins | Serves: 2

Ingredients:
- US: 400g canned tomatoes, 200ml vegetable broth, 1 onion (chopped), 2 garlic cloves (minced), 30ml olive oil, 2 slices bread, 50g cheddar cheese (grated), salt, and pepper
- UK: 400g canned tomatoes, 200ml vegetable broth, 1 onion (chopped), 2 garlic cloves (minced), 30ml olive oil, 2 slices bread, 50g cheddar cheese (grated), salt, and pepper

Instructions:
1. In a saucepan, heat the olive oil and sauté the onion and garlic until soft.
2. Add the canned tomatoes and vegetable broth, then simmer for 10 minutes.
3. Use a blender to puree the soup until smooth, seasoning with salt and pepper.
4. Meanwhile, grill the bread with cheese until golden and melty.
5. Serve the soup with the grilled cheese on the side!

Nutritional Info: Calories: 300 | Fat: 15g | Carbs: 30g | Protein: 12g

Note: Add herbs for extra flavour!

Breakfast Burrito Bowl

Prep: 10 mins | Cook: 10 mins | Serves: 2

Ingredients:
- US: 200g cooked rice, 4 large eggs, 100g black beans (canned), 100g salsa, 50g avocado (sliced), 30ml olive oil, salt, and pepper
- UK: 200g cooked rice, 4 large eggs, 100g black beans (canned), 100g salsa, 50g avocado (sliced), 30ml olive oil, salt, and pepper

Instructions:
1. In a frying pan, heat the olive oil and scramble the eggs with salt and pepper.
2. In bowls, layer cooked rice, black beans, scrambled eggs, and salsa.
3. Top with avocado slices and enjoy your Breakfast Burrito Bowl!

Nutritional Info: Calories: 400 | Fat: 20g | Carbs: 40g | Protein: 15g

Note: Feel free to add cheese or jalapeños for extra kick!

Kitchen Sink Stir Fry

Prep: 10 mins | Cook: 15 mins | Serves: 2

Ingredients:
- US: 200g mixed vegetables (frozen or fresh), 200g cooked protein (chicken, tofu, etc.), 30ml soy sauce, 30ml olive oil, 1 teaspoon garlic (minced), 1 teaspoon ginger (minced), 150g cooked rice
- UK: 200g mixed vegetables (frozen or fresh), 200g cooked protein (chicken, tofu, etc.), 30ml soy sauce, 30ml olive oil, 1 teaspoon garlic (minced), 1 teaspoon ginger (minced), 150g cooked rice

Instructions:
1. Heat the olive oil in a large frying pan or wok over medium-high heat.
2. Add the minced garlic and ginger, cooking for about 30 seconds until fragrant.
3. Toss in the mixed vegetables and stir-fry for 5-7 minutes until they are tender.
4. Add the cooked protein and soy sauce, stirring well to combine everything.
5. Serve over a bed of cooked rice, and enjoy your Kitchen Sink Stir Fry!

Nutritional Info: Calories: 450 | Fat: 15g | Carbs: 55g | Protein: 25g

Note: Use any leftover veggies or proteins you have; it's super versatile!

Leftover Veg Frittata

Prep: 5 mins | Cook: 20 mins | Serves: 2

Ingredients:
- US: 4 large eggs, 100g leftover vegetables (chopped), 30ml milk, 50g cheese (grated), salt, and pepper
- UK: 4 large eggs, 100g leftover vegetables (chopped), 30ml milk, 50g cheese (grated), salt, and pepper

Instructions:
1. Preheat your oven to 180°C (350°F).
2. In a bowl, whisk together the eggs, milk, salt, and pepper until well combined.
3. Stir in the chopped vegetables and cheese.
4. Pour the mixture into a greased oven-safe frying pan.
5. Cook on the stovetop for 3-4 minutes until the edges start to set.
6. Transfer to the oven and bake for about 15 minutes, or until the frittata is set in the middle.
7. Slice and serve warm!

Nutritional Info: Calories: 300 | Fat: 20g | Carbs: 5g | Protein: 20g

Note: This is a fantastic way to use up any leftover veggies you have lying around!

Clean-Out-The-Cupboard Curry

Prep: 10 mins | Cook: 30 mins | Serves: 4

Ingredients:
- US: 1 can (400g) chickpeas (drained), 1 can (400g) diced tomatoes, 1 onion (chopped), 2 garlic cloves (minced), 1 tablespoon curry powder, 30ml olive oil, 200ml vegetable broth, 100g frozen peas, salt, and pepper
- UK: 1 can (400g) chickpeas (drained), 1 can (400g) diced tomatoes, 1 onion (chopped), 2 garlic cloves (minced), 1 tablespoon curry powder, 30ml olive oil, 200ml vegetable broth, 100g frozen peas, salt, and pepper

Instructions:
1. In a pot, heat the olive oil over medium heat and sauté the onion and garlic until soft.
2. Add the curry powder and cook for another minute to release the flavours.
3. Stir in the chickpeas, diced tomatoes, and vegetable broth.
4. Bring to a simmer and cook for 20 minutes, adding the peas in the last 5 minutes.
5. Season with salt and pepper to taste and serve hot with rice or bread.

Nutritional Info: Calories: 350 | Fat: 10g | Carbs: 55g | Protein: 15g

Note: Feel free to add any other canned goods or leftover veggies!

End-of-Term Pasta Bake

Prep: 10 mins | Cook: 30 mins | Serves: 4

Ingredients:
- US: 300g pasta (any shape), 200g leftover cooked meat (optional), 1 can (400g) tomato sauce, 50g cheese (grated), 1 tablespoon Italian herbs, salt, and pepper
- UK: 300g pasta (any shape), 200g leftover cooked meat (optional), 1 can (400g) tomato sauce, 50g cheese (grated), 1 tablespoon Italian herbs, salt, and pepper

Instructions:
1. Preheat your oven to 180°C (350°F).
2. Cook the pasta according to package instructions until al dente. Drain and return to the pot.
3. Stir in the tomato sauce, leftover meat (if using), herbs, salt, and pepper.
4. Transfer the mixture to a baking dish and sprinkle cheese on top.
5. Bake for 20-25 minutes until bubbly and golden on top.
6. Serve hot and enjoy your hearty pasta bake!

Nutritional Info: Calories: 450 | Fat: 15g | Carbs: 65g | Protein: 20g

Note: You can add any leftover vegetables to boost nutrition!

Fridge-Raid Fried Rice

Prep: 5 mins | Cook: 10 mins | Serves: 2

Ingredients:
- US: 200g cooked rice, 2 eggs, 100g leftover vegetables (chopped), 30ml soy sauce, 30ml sesame oil, 1 green onion (chopped)
- UK: 200g cooked rice, 2 eggs, 100g leftover vegetables (chopped), 30ml soy sauce, 30ml sesame oil, 1 spring onion (chopped)

Instructions:
1. Heat sesame oil in a large frying pan over medium heat.
2. Scramble the eggs in the pan and set aside when cooked.
3. Add leftover vegetables to the pan and stir-fry for a couple of minutes.
4. Add the cooked rice and soy sauce, mixing well to combine everything.
5. Stir in the scrambled eggs and chopped green onion before serving.
6. Enjoy your Fridge-Raid Fried Rice!

Nutritional Info: Calories: 400 | Fat: 15g | Carbs: 50g | Protein: 12g

Pantry Staple Soup

Prep: 5 mins | Cook: 20 mins | Serves: 4

Ingredients:
- US: 1 can (400g) lentils (drained), 1 can (400g) diced tomatoes, 1 onion (chopped), 2 garlic cloves (minced), 500ml vegetable broth, 1 tablespoon olive oil, 1 teaspoon dried herbs, salt, and pepper
- UK: 1 can (400g) lentils (drained), 1 can (400g) diced tomatoes, 1 onion (chopped), 2 garlic cloves (minced), 500ml vegetable broth, 1 tablespoon olive oil, 1 teaspoon dried herbs, salt, and pepper

Instructions:
1. In a large pot, heat the olive oil over medium heat and sauté the onion and garlic until soft.
2. Add the lentils, diced tomatoes, vegetable broth, and dried herbs.
3. Bring to a simmer and cook for 15 minutes, stirring occasionally.
4. Blend if you prefer a smooth soup, or leave it chunky.
5. Season with salt and pepper to taste before serving hot!

Nutritional Info: Calories: 250 | Fat: 5g | Carbs: 40g | Protein: 15g

Note: Perfect for using up those canned goods!

Anything Goes Quesadillas

Prep: 5 mins | Cook: 10 mins | Serves: 2

Ingredients:
- US: 4 tortillas, 200g cheese (grated), 100g leftover meat or veggies, 30ml olive oil, salsa (for serving)
- UK: 4 tortillas, 200g cheese (grated), 100g leftover meat or veggies, 30ml olive oil, salsa (for serving)

Instructions:
1. Heat olive oil in a frying pan over medium heat.
2. Place a tortilla in the pan and sprinkle half with cheese and your choice of fillings.
3. Fold the tortilla in half and cook for about 3-4 minutes on each side until golden and crispy.
4. Remove from the pan and cut into wedges.
5. Serve with salsa and enjoy your Anything Goes Quesadillas!

Nutritional Info: Calories: 450 | Fat: 25g | Carbs: 40g | Protein: 20g

Note: Use any cheese and fillings you have on hand!

Last-Minute Noodle Bowl

Prep: 5 mins | Cook: 10 mins | Serves: 2

Ingredients:
- US: 200g noodles (any type), 100g leftover veggies, 100g cooked protein (optional), 30ml soy sauce, 30ml sesame oil, 1 teaspoon sriracha (optional)
- UK: 200g noodles (any type), 100g leftover veggies, 100g cooked protein (optional), 30ml soy sauce, 30ml sesame oil, 1 teaspoon sriracha (optional)

Instructions:
1. Cook the noodles according to package instructions and drain.
2. In a pan, heat sesame oil over medium heat and stir-fry the leftover veggies and protein for 2-3 minutes.
3. Add the cooked noodles and soy sauce, mixing everything well.
4. Serve hot with a drizzle of sriracha if you like it spicy!

Nutritional Info: Calories: 400 | Fat: 10g | Carbs: 60g | Protein: 20g

Note: A quick meal for when you're in a rush!

Scraps Smoothie

Prep: 5 mins | Cook: 0 mins | Serves: 2

Ingredients:
- US: 1 banana, 100g leftover fruit (berries, apples, etc.), 200ml yogurt or milk, 30ml honey (optional), ice cubes (optional)
- UK: 1 banana, 100g leftover fruit (berries, apples, etc.), 200ml yogurt or milk, 30ml honey (optional), ice cubes (optional)

Instructions:
1. In a blender, combine the banana, leftover fruit, yogurt or milk, and honey.
2. Blend until smooth, adding ice cubes for a chilled smoothie if desired.
3. Pour into glasses and enjoy your Scraps Smoothie!

Nutritional Info: Calories: 250 | Fat: 5g | Carbs: 45g | Protein: 8g

Note: A great way to use up any fruits before they go bad!

Cleanout Chilli

Prep: 10 mins | Cook: 30 mins | Serves: 4

Ingredients:
- US: 1 can (400g) kidney beans (drained), 1 can (400g) diced tomatoes, 1 onion (chopped), 2 garlic cloves (minced), 1 tablespoon chili powder, 30ml olive oil, 500ml vegetable broth, salt, and pepper
- UK: 1 can (400g) kidney beans (drained), 1 can (400g) diced tomatoes, 1 onion (chopped), 2 garlic cloves (minced), 1 tablespoon chili powder, 30ml olive oil, 500ml vegetable broth, salt, and pepper

Instructions:
1. Heat the olive oil in a pot over medium heat and sauté the onion and garlic until soft.
2. Add the chili powder and cook for 1 minute to toast the spices.
3. Stir in the kidney beans, diced tomatoes, and vegetable broth.
4. Bring to a simmer and cook for 20 minutes, seasoning with salt and pepper to taste.
5. Serve hot with bread or rice!

Nutritional Info: Calories: 350 | Fat: 10g | Carbs: 50g | Protein: 15g

Note: Use any leftover beans or vegetables to customise your chilli!

Microwave Mug Cake (3 Flavours)

Prep: 5 mins | Cook: 1 min | Serves: 1

Ingredients:

- US: 4 tablespoons all-purpose flour, 4 tablespoons sugar, 2 tablespoons cocoa powder (for chocolate), or 1 mashed banana (for banana), or 2 tablespoons peanut butter (for peanut butter), 1/8 teaspoon baking powder, 3 tablespoons milk, 2 tablespoons vegetable oil, optional toppings: chocolate chips, nuts, or whipped cream
- UK: 4 tablespoons plain flour, 4 tablespoons sugar, 2 tablespoons cocoa powder (for chocolate), or 1 mashed banana (for banana), or 2 tablespoons peanut butter (for peanut butter), 1/8 teaspoon baking powder, 3 tablespoons milk, 2 tablespoons vegetable oil, optional toppings: chocolate chips, nuts, or whipped cream

Instructions:

1. In a large microwave-safe mug, mix the flour, sugar, cocoa powder (if using), and baking powder.
2. Add the milk and vegetable oil, stirring until smooth. If making banana or peanut butter flavour, mix in the banana or peanut butter at this stage.
3. Microwave on high for about 1 minute (microwave times may vary). Check if it's cooked through; if not, microwave in 10-second bursts until done.
4. Allow to cool slightly, then top with your favourite toppings and enjoy your cake straight from the mug!

Nutritional Info (Chocolate): Calories: 350 | Fat: 18g | Carbs: 40g | Protein: 5g

Note: Feel free to experiment with different flavours!

No-Bake Energy Balls

Prep: 10 mins | Cook: 0 mins | Serves: 12

Ingredients:

- US: 200g rolled oats, 100g nut butter (peanut, almond, etc.), 50g honey or maple syrup, 50g chocolate chips or dried fruit, optional: 30g chia seeds or flaxseeds
- UK: 200g rolled oats, 100g nut butter (peanut, almond, etc.), 50g honey or maple syrup, 50g chocolate chips or dried fruit, optional: 30g chia seeds or flaxseeds

Instructions:

1. In a large bowl, combine the rolled oats, nut butter, honey, and any optional ingredients.
2. Mix until well combined. If the mixture is too dry, add a bit more nut butter or honey.
3. Roll the mixture into small balls (about the size of a golf ball).
4. Place the energy balls on a tray and refrigerate for at least 30 minutes to firm up.
5. Enjoy these tasty bites whenever you need a quick energy boost!

Nutritional Info (per ball): Calories: 100 | Fat: 5g | Carbs: 10g | Protein: 3g

Note: These can be stored in the fridge for up to a week.

Easy Chocolate Brownies

Prep: 10 mins | Cook: 20 mins | Serves: 9

Ingredients:
- US: 200g dark chocolate (chopped), 100g unsalted butter, 150g sugar, 3 large eggs, 100g all-purpose flour, 1/2 teaspoon vanilla extract, optional: 50g nuts (chopped)
- UK: 200g dark chocolate (chopped), 100g unsalted butter, 150g sugar, 3 large eggs, 100g plain flour, 1/2 teaspoon vanilla extract, optional: 50g nuts (chopped)

Instructions:
1. Preheat your oven to 180°C (350°F) and grease a baking tray.
2. In a heatproof bowl, melt the chocolate and butter together (you can do this in the microwave in 30-second intervals).
3. Once melted, stir in the sugar and let it cool slightly.
4. Beat in the eggs one at a time, then add the flour and vanilla extract. Mix until smooth.
5. If using, fold in the nuts, then pour the batter into the prepared tray.
6. Bake for 20-25 minutes until a toothpick inserted in the centre comes out slightly moist.
7. Let cool, cut into squares, and enjoy your fudgy brownies!

Nutritional Info (per brownie): Calories: 200 | Fat: 10g | Carbs: 25g | Protein: 3g

Note: You can add chocolate chips for extra indulgence!

Fruit Crumble for One

Prep: 5 mins | Cook: 20 mins | Serves: 1

Ingredients:
- US: 150g mixed fruit (frozen or fresh, like berries or apples), 20g sugar (for the fruit), 40g oats, 20g flour, 30g butter (cold), 10g sugar (for the crumble)
- UK: 150g mixed fruit (frozen or fresh, like berries or apples), 20g sugar (for the fruit), 40g oats, 20g plain flour, 30g butter (cold), 10g sugar (for the crumble)

Instructions:
1. Preheat your oven to 180°C (350°F).
2. In a small oven-safe dish, mix the fruit with 20g of sugar and set aside.
3. In a bowl, combine the oats, flour, and 10g of sugar.
4. Cut in the cold butter using your fingers until the mixture resembles breadcrumbs.
5. Spread the crumble topping over the fruit mixture.
6. Bake for 20 minutes until golden brown and bubbly.
7. Serve warm, perhaps with a scoop of ice cream!

Nutritional Info: Calories: 300 | Fat: 15g | Carbs: 40g | Protein: 5g

Note: This is a great way to use up any leftover fruit!

Two-Ingredient Banana Pancakes

Prep: 5 mins | Cook: 5 mins | Serves: 2

Ingredients:
- US: 1 ripe banana (mashed), 2 large eggs
- UK: 1 ripe banana (mashed), 2 large eggs

Instructions:
1. In a bowl, mash the banana well.
2. Beat in the eggs until fully combined.
3. Heat a non-stick frying pan over medium heat and add a small amount of oil.
4. Pour small portions of the batter into the pan and cook for about 1-2 minutes on each side until golden brown.
5. Serve with your favourite toppings, such as honey or maple syrup!

Nutritional Info (per pancake): Calories: 70 | Fat: 3g | Carbs: 10g | Protein: 3g

Homemade Ice Lollies

Prep: 5 mins | Cook: 0 mins | Serves: 4
Ingredients:
- US: 300ml fruit juice (your choice), 150g fresh fruit (berries, chopped fruit)
- UK: 300ml fruit juice (your choice), 150g fresh fruit (berries, chopped fruit)

Instructions:
1. In a bowl, mix the fruit juice with the fresh fruit.
2. Pour the mixture into ice lolly molds, leaving a little space at the top.
3. Insert the sticks and freeze for at least 4 hours or until solid.
4. To release, run the molds under warm water for a few seconds.
5. Enjoy your refreshing homemade ice lollies!

Nutritional Info (per lolly): Calories: 50 | Fat: 0g | Carbs: 12g | Protein: 1g
Note: These are a great way to stay cool in the summer!

Quick Cheesecake in a Glass

Prep: 10 mins | Cook: 0 mins | Serves: 2
Ingredients:
- US: 200g cream cheese, 50g sugar, 1 teaspoon vanilla extract, 150g digestive biscuits (crushed), 50g butter (melted), 100g fruit or fruit sauce (for topping)
- UK: 200g cream cheese, 50g sugar, 1 teaspoon vanilla extract, 150g digestive biscuits (crushed), 50g butter (melted), 100g fruit or fruit sauce (for topping)

Instructions:
1. In a bowl, mix the cream cheese, sugar, and vanilla extract until smooth.
2. In another bowl, combine the crushed biscuits with the melted butter.
3. Layer the biscuit mixture in the bottom of serving glasses.
4. Add a layer of the cream cheese mixture on top.
5. Top with your choice of fruit or fruit sauce.
6. Chill in the fridge for at least 30 minutes before serving.

Nutritional Info (per glass): Calories: 250 | Fat: 15g | Carbs: 30g | Protein: 4g
Note: This dessert is perfect for quick entertaining!

Microwave Cinnamon Roll

Prep: 5 mins | Cook: 1 min | Serves: 1
Ingredients:
- US: 4 tablespoons all-purpose flour, 1 tablespoon sugar, 1/2 teaspoon baking powder, 1/4 teaspoon salt, 1 tablespoon milk, 1 tablespoon vegetable oil, 1/2 teaspoon cinnamon, optional: icing for drizzling
- UK: 4 tablespoons plain flour, 1 tablespoon sugar, 1/2 teaspoon baking powder, 1/4 teaspoon salt, 1 tablespoon milk, 1 tablespoon vegetable oil, 1/2 teaspoon cinnamon, optional: icing for drizzling

Instructions:
1. In a microwave-safe bowl, mix the flour, sugar, baking powder, and salt.
2. Add the milk and oil, stirring until combined.
3. Sprinkle the cinnamon over the top and gently swirl it in.
4. Microwave on high for 1 minute. Check if it's cooked through; if not, microwave for an additional 10-15 seconds.
5. Drizzle with icing if desired and enjoy your cinnamon roll!

Nutritional Info: Calories: 300 | Fat: 15g | Carbs: 40g | Protein: 5g
Note: A perfect treat for a cozy morning!

Nutella-Stuffed Cookies

Prep: 15 mins | Cook: 10 mins | Serves: 12

Ingredients:
- US: 200g all-purpose flour, 100g unsalted butter (softened), 100g sugar, 1 large egg, 1 teaspoon vanilla extract, 100g Nutella, 1/2 teaspoon baking soda, 1/4 teaspoon salt
- UK: 200g plain flour, 100g unsalted butter (softened), 100g sugar, 1 large egg, 1 teaspoon vanilla extract, 100g Nutella, 1/2 teaspoon baking soda, 1/4 teaspoon salt

Instructions:
1. Preheat your oven to 180°C (350°F) and line a baking tray with parchment paper.
2. In a mixing bowl, cream together the softened butter and sugar until light and fluffy.
3. Beat in the egg and vanilla extract until well combined.
4. In another bowl, whisk together the flour, baking soda, and salt. Gradually add this to the wet ingredients, mixing until just combined.
5. Take a tablespoon of dough, flatten it, and place a teaspoon of Nutella in the centre. Wrap the dough around the Nutella and roll into a ball.
6. Place the cookie balls on the baking tray and bake for about 10 minutes, or until the edges are golden.
7. Let them cool for a few minutes before devouring these gooey delights!

Nutritional Info (per cookie): Calories: 150 | Fat: 7g | Carbs: 20g | Protein: 2g

Note: Keep an eye on them; the softer they are, the more delicious!

Healthy Frozen Yogurt Bark

Prep: 10 mins | Cook: 0 mins | Serves: 4

Ingredients:
- US: 400g Greek yogurt, 2 tablespoons honey or maple syrup, 100g mixed berries (fresh or frozen), 30g nuts (chopped) or granola (optional)
- UK: 400g Greek yogurt, 2 tablespoons honey or maple syrup, 100g mixed berries (fresh or frozen), 30g nuts (chopped) or granola (optional)

Instructions:
1. Line a baking tray with parchment paper.
2. In a mixing bowl, combine the Greek yogurt and honey (or maple syrup) until smooth.
3. Spread the yogurt mixture evenly onto the lined baking tray.
4. Sprinkle the mixed berries and nuts (or granola) over the top.
5. Freeze for at least 2 hours until solid.
6. Once frozen, break into pieces and enjoy your refreshing treat!

Nutritional Info (per serving): Calories: 120 | Fat: 4g | Carbs: 15g | Protein: 6g

Note: This is a great way to cool down on a hot day!

ADDITIONAL RESOURCES

CONVERSION CHARTS

Volume Conversions
- ❖ 1 cup = 240ml = 16 tablespoons
- ❖ 1 tablespoon = 15ml = 3 teaspoons
- ❖ 1 teaspoon = 5ml
- ❖ 1 pint (UK) = 568ml
- ❖ 1 pint (US) = 473ml

Weight Conversions
- ❖ 1 ounce = 28g
- ❖ 1 pound = 454g
- ❖ 1 kg = 2.2 pounds

Temperature Guide
- ❖ Very low: 120°C/250°F/Gas Mark ½
- ❖ Low: 150°C/300°F/Gas Mark 2
- ❖ Moderate: 180°C/350°F/Gas Mark 4
- ❖ Hot: 200°C/400°F/Gas Mark 6
- ❖ Very hot: 220°C/425°F/Gas Mark 7

Ingredient Substitution Guide
Baking Emergencies
When you're mid-recipe and realize you're missing something:
Eggs
- 1 egg = 1 mashed banana (in sweet recipes)
- 1 egg = 60ml applesauce
- 1 egg = 1 tbsp ground flaxseed + 3 tbsp water
- 1 egg = 60ml yogurt

Milk
- 1 cup milk = 1 cup water + 1 tbsp butter
- 1 cup milk = 1 cup soy/almond/oat milk
- 1 cup buttermilk = 1 cup milk + 1 tbsp lemon juice

Flour
- 1 cup self-raising flour = 1 cup plain flour + 2 tsp baking powder
- 1 cup bread flour = 1 cup plain flour + 1 tbsp vital wheat gluten
- 1 cup plain flour = 1 cup cornflour (for gluten-free thickening)

Cooking Substitutions
Herbs & Spices
- 1 tbsp fresh herbs = 1 tsp dried herbs
- 1 clove garlic = ¼ tsp garlic powder
- 1 inch ginger = 1 tsp ground ginger
- 1 onion = 1 tbsp onion powder

Cooking Liquids
- 1 cup stock = 1 cup water + 1 stock cube
- 1 cup wine = 1 cup stock + 1 tbsp vinegar
- 1 cup cream = 1 cup milk + 1 tbsp butter

Basic Flavour Pairing Guide
Classic Combinations
Tried and tested pairs that always work:

- Tomato + Basil
- Lemon + Garlic
- Beef + Rosemary
- Chicken + Thyme
- Pork + Apple
- Fish + Lemon
- Lamb + Mint
- Chocolate + Orange
- Strawberry + Vanilla
- Mushroom + Thyme

Cuisine Quick-Start Guides
Italian Basics
- Garlic + Olive Oil + Basil
- Tomato + Oregano + Parmesan

Mushroom + Thyme + White Wine
Indian Essentials
- Cumin + Coriander + Turmeric
- Ginger + Garlic + Onion
- Cardamom + Cinnamon + Clove

Chinese Fundamentals
- Soy Sauce + Ginger + Garlic
- Five Spice + Star Anise + Cinnamon
- Sesame Oil + Spring Onion + Garlic

Tips for Hosting Flat Dinners and Parties
Planning Your First Dinner Party
Because microwave meals won't impress anyone:
Timeline Planning
1. Two Days Before:
- Plan menu
- Make shopping list
- Check dietary restrictions
- Confirm guest numbers
2. Day Before:
- Shopping
- Prep ingredients
- Clean communal areas
- Chill drinks
3. Day Of:
- Final shopping
- Start cooking
- Set up space
- Welcome guests

Party Food Planning
Calculate portions like a pro:
- Snacks: 4-5 pieces per person
- Main dish: 250g per person
- Side dishes: 100g per person
- Dessert: One portion per person
- Drinks: 2-3 drinks per person for first 2 hours

Dealing with Dietary Restrictions in a Shared Kitchen

Common Restrictions Guide

How to handle different dietary needs:

Vegetarian
- Separate chopping boards
- Check ingredients (watch for gelatin, rennet)
- Label shared items clearly
- Keep veggie foods on top shelf

Vegan
- Check all ingredients
- Watch for hidden animal products
- Label personal items
- Use separate utensils for cooking

Gluten-Free
- Clean surfaces thoroughly
- Use separate toaster
- Check all ingredients
- Store GF items separately

Cross-Contamination Prevention
- Use different utensils
- Clean surfaces between prep
- Store foods separately
- Label everything clearly

Quick Guide to Herbs and Spices

Essential Herbs

Fresh Herbs
- Basil: Italian dishes, tomato-based recipes
- Coriander: Asian and Mexican dishes
- Mint: Middle Eastern, drinks, desserts
- Parsley: Universal garnish, stocks
- Rosemary: Roasts, potatoes, bread

Dried Herbs
- Oregano: Italian, Greek dishes
- Thyme: Soups, stews, roasts
- Bay Leaves: Stocks, stews
- Mixed Herbs: General cooking

Basic Spices

Everyday Spices
- Black Pepper: Everything
- Cumin: Mexican, Indian dishes
- Paprika: Color, mild heat
- Chili Powder: Heat control
- Cinnamon: Sweet and savory
- Spice Blends
- Italian Seasoning
- Curry Powder
- Chinese Five Spice
- Taco Seasoning
- Garam Masala

HOW TO STOCK A STUDENT BAR FOR PARTIES

Essential Equipment
- ✓ Measuring jigger
- ✓ Shaker
- ✓ Strainer
- ✓ Bottle opener
- ✓ Corkscrew
- ✓ Ice bucket
- ✓ Basic glassware

Basic Spirits
- ✓ Vodka
- ✓ Gin
- ✓ White Rum
- ✓ Tequila
- ✓ Whiskey
- ✓ Mixers

Don't forget:
- ✓ Tonic Water
- ✓ Cola
- ✓ Lemonade
- ✓ Cranberry Juice
- ✓ Orange Juice
- ✓ Soda Water

Simple Party Cocktails
- ✓ Gin & Tonic
- ✓ Vodka Cranberry
- ✓ Rum & Cola
- ✓ Tequila Sunrise
- ✓ Moscow Mule

CLEANING AND MAINTAINING YOUR KITCHEN SPACE

Daily Cleaning Routine

Quick tasks to keep things manageable:

1. Wipe surfaces after use
2. Wash dishes/load dishwasher
3. Sweep floor
4. Take out full bins
5. Clean spills immediately

Weekly Deep Clean

The bigger jobs:

1. Clean microwave
2. Scrub stovetop
3. Mop floors
4. Clean fridge shelves
5. Descale kettle
6. Clean oven (if needed)

Monthly Maintenance

Don't forget these:

1. Deep clean oven
2. Clear drains
3. Clean cupboard interiors
4. Check for expired foods
5. Clean small appliances

Cleaning Product Essentials

Stock these basics:

- Multi-surface cleaner
- Dish soap
- Sponges/cloths
- Floor cleaner
- Drain cleaner
- Oven cleaner
- Bin bags

CONCLUSION

Congratulations! You've made it through your Student Cookbook, and hopefully by now, your kitchen has become more than just a place to heat up instant noodles. Whether you've mastered the art of meal prep, conquered the challenge of cooking on a budget, or successfully hosted your first dinner party, you've taken important steps in your culinary journey.

Remember when you first started? Maybe you were intimidated by the thought of cooking from scratch, or perhaps you were convinced that good food had to be expensive or complicated. Now you know better. You've learned that with a few basic ingredients, some simple techniques, and a dash of creativity, you can create delicious, nutritious meals that won't break the bank or take up your entire evening.

The recipes in this book are more than just instructions – they're building blocks for your cooking confidence. From the basic "Empty the Fridge" specials to impressive date night dinners, each recipe has taught you something valuable about flavors, techniques, and kitchen management. These skills will serve you well beyond your student years.

Some key takeaways to remember:

> ➤ Good cooking doesn't require expensive ingredients or fancy equipment
> ➤ Planning ahead saves both time and money
> ➤ Mistakes are normal and are actually great learning opportunities
> ➤ Simple dishes, well-prepared, are often the most satisfying
> ➤ Sharing food with friends creates some of the best university memories

As you continue your culinary adventures, don't be afraid to experiment and make these recipes your own. Add different spices, swap ingredients, or combine ideas from different recipes. The best cooks are those who aren't afraid to try new things and learn from both successes and failures.

And speaking of failures – embrace them! That slightly burnt toast, the oversalted soup, or the pasta that turned to mush – these are all badges of honor in your cooking journey. Every experienced cook has a story about kitchen disasters that eventually became valuable lessons. Remember to keep this cookbook handy even after your student days. These budget-friendly, time-saving recipes and techniques will be useful whether you're starting your first job, moving into your own place, or cooking for a family someday. Good cooking habits, like preparing healthy meals and managing your food budget, are life skills that will always serve you well.

Finally, thank you for letting this cookbook be part of your student experience. Cooking is one of the most valuable life skills you can develop during your university years, and it's been our pleasure to guide you through it. Keep cooking, keep learning, and most importantly, keep enjoying the process of creating delicious meals for yourself and others.

Now, get back in that kitchen and start cooking! Your next culinary adventure awaits.

Bon appétit!

Printed in Dunstable, United Kingdom